Pawsitivity Unleashed

UNLEASHING LIFE LESSONS

Memoir Edition

A Journey to Rediscover, Reinvent, & Reclaim Your
Life with purpose and Passion

Kristin Leest

Pawsitivity Unleashed

Published by Pawsitivity, LLC

Pawsitivity Unleashed: Unleashing Life Lessons Memoir Edition

ISBN: 9798224628841

Cover design by Al Mahmud

Cover illustration by Al Mahmud

Editing by Kristin Leest

Interior design by Kristin Leest

Printed in United States

For permissions requests, please contact Pawsitivity, LLC at kristinleest@gmail.com

www.kristinleest.com

First Edition

Pawsitivity Unleashed

Heidi, and Ryan (my son aged three) when we first
adopted her.

"Not all who wander are lost."

-J.R.R. Tolkien

Pawsitivity Unleashed

UNLEASHING LIFE LESSONS

Memoir Edition

A Journey to Rediscover, Reinvent, & Reclaim Your Life with purpose and Passion

Kristin Leest

Dedication

To My Beloved Furry Companion, Heidi,

You have been my faithful companion, my source of joy, and my guiding light. Through your unwavering loyalty, boundless love, and endless patience, you have enriched my life in ways I could never have imagined. This book I dedicate to you, my cherished friend, for inspiring me, comforting me, and reminding me of the true meaning of unconditional love. Thank you for being my constant companion on this journey called life.

Table of Contents

Pawsitivity Unleashed

Pawsitivity Unleashed

Acknowledgments

I would like to express my heartfelt gratitude to everyone who has contributed to the creation of this book. First, I want to thank my furry mentor, Heidi, whose presence has been an endless source of inspiration and wisdom. Your unwavering support and unconditional love have guided me through this journey of self-discovery.

I am deeply grateful to my family and friends for their encouragement, understanding, and unwavering belief in me. Your patience, love, and support have been my rock during the difficulties of authoring this book.

A special thank you to my editor, whose keen eye and insightful feedback have helped shape this book into its final form. Your dedication and expertise have been invaluable throughout the writing process.

I am also indebted to the countless life coaches and mental health professionals whose wisdom and knowledge have provided insight into the content of this book. Your contributions have enriched its pages and inspired me to continue learning and growing.

Lastly, I would like to thank the readers who have joined me on this journey of discovery. Your interest, enthusiasm, and support mean the world to me, and I hope that this book brings you as much joy and inspiration as it has brought me.

Thank you all sincerely.

Warm regards,

Kristin

Foreword

Welcome to "Pawsitivity Unleashed: A Journey to Purpose & Passion. It brings me immense joy and anticipation to begin this journey with you, where I will share about my transformative path to success, self-discovery, and growth. Here, you will not only discover my passion for dogs and dog training, but we will also explore my personal story in a unique and inspiring way.

Within these pages, you will accompany me through the beginnings of my journey, laying the foundation for what was to come. We will navigate through the challenges I encountered and the pivotal moments that led to my "unraveling," a process that led me to find my catalyst for profound change and success. Together, we will explore how these experiences shaped my perspective and propelled me forward on this journey of reinvention and self-discovery.

Here I share with you the wisdom and tools I have gathered through years of personal exploration and professional experience. These tried, tested, and proven resources are now consolidated into the 30-day challenge—an opportunity to reinvent, rediscover, and reclaim your life.

Pawsitivity Unleashed

These invaluable resources have become the guiding principles of my life, helping me overcome my own struggles and those of my clients. Many of us have felt trapped in cycles of unfulfilling routines and responsibilities, leading to a sense of stagnation and a lack of purpose. Through this challenge, I offer you the chance to break free from these constraints and step into a life of renewed energy and purpose.

In this memoir, I share the "who, what, where, when, and why" of my personal journey to success. You will find additional tips, insights, and stories that will inspire and motivate you. Accompanying this memoir is a coordinating workbook and journal—the "how" of your transformational journey. This workbook serves as your resource guide, offering practical exercises and prompts to help you apply these principles to your own life.

If you share my love for dogs and find yourself struggling with similar challenges, this book and workbook are tailor-made for you. Together, we will explore how to integrate these tools and insights into your daily life, creating positive change and lasting transformation.

During my own journey, I discovered the power of replacing old habits with new, healthy ones. Practices such as journaling, reading books on self-reflection, mindfulness meditation, therapy, self-reflection worksheets, seeking feedback from peers, artistic expression, podcast listening, and utilizing self-reflection apps—all these contributed to my personal growth and success.

As a dog trainer, entrepreneur, mother, and more, I have experienced first-hand how these tools can enhance productivity, expand abilities, and skyrocket success. In this challenge, I will guide you on how to incorporate these practices into your own life, empowering you to create the life you desire.

My personal journey has been a winding path, leading me to discover my deep passion for dogs. This passion inspired me to pursue a career as a dog trainer, where I found a profound interest in the health and wellness of both dogs and people alike. It was this journey that also led me to a transformative personal experience—I embarked on a health and wellness journey myself, shedding over eighty pounds.

But my journey does not stop there. Fueled by a desire to make a positive impact, I decided to act. I founded a non-profit organization dedicated to helping children in need, channeling my passion for giving back into meaningful projects that uplift communities.

Additionally, my love for dogs and my commitment to their well-being inspired me to create a natural nutritional dog supplement company. This endeavor not only allows me to share my passion for canine health but also gives back to the animal community.

Pawsitivity Unleashed

I am proud to say that 1% of all our sales go towards supporting dogs and cats in animal rescues and shelters.

Through these endeavors, I have found purpose and fulfillment in making a difference, both in the lives of animals and in the communities around me. My journey has been one of growth, passion, and giving back, and I am excited to continue this path of creating positive change.

When it comes to the journey of life, it mirrors the twists, turns, challenges, and triumphs we encounter along the way. Often, we find ourselves in pursuit of meaning, purpose, and fulfillment, only to be overwhelmed by the complexities of modern living. It was during a period of deep introspection and soul-searching that I began my own transformative journey, with my steadfast companion Heidi by my side.

In the pages of "Pawsitivity Unleashed," I extend a heartfelt invitation for you to join me on a 30-day adventure of self-discovery, guided by the wisdom and companionship of our furry friends. Through daily reflections, exercises, and practical tips, we will explore how to harness the power of "pawsitivity" to rediscover your passions, reinvent yourself, and reclaim your life with purpose and joy.

Drawing from my personal experiences and the insights gleaned from collaborating with numerous individuals on their quest for a more fulfilling life, I offer you a roadmap to personal growth and transformation. With a unique perspective shaped by my background as a dog trainer, I warmly invite you to begin this journey with me.

Together, we will discuss the profound insights that our beloved canine companions offer us. From them, we learn invaluable lessons in resilience, gratitude, and the boundless capacity for unconditional love. Through the lens of a dog trainer's mindset, we will explore how these teachings can be applied to navigate the challenges of our own lives with grace and courage.

Join me as we uncover the parallels between the teachings of our furry friends and the paths to personal fulfillment. Let us embrace the wisdom of dogs as we embark on this transformative journey together.

As you step into each day of this 30-day adventure, I encourage you to approach it with an open heart and a curious mind. Embrace the possibilities that lie ahead, knowing that the path to self-discovery may not always be easy. However, with dedication, perseverance, and the unwavering support of your furry mentor, you possess the power to create a life filled with purpose, passion, and joy.

I am deeply honored to be your guide on this transformative journey, and I eagerly anticipate witnessing the incredible growth and change that awaits you. May "Pawsitivity Unleashed" serve as

Pawsitivity Unleashed

hope and inspiration, guiding you toward a life of greater meaning, connection, and fulfillment.

With warmest regards,

Kristin

Introduction

As I hold "Pawsitivity Unleashed: A 30-Day Journey to Rediscover, Reinvent, and Reclaim Your Life" in my hands, it is surreal to think about the transformative impact it is about to have – both on your life and mine.

For years, I grappled with a sense of unease, questioning why my achievements left me feeling hollow, why my dreams seemed just out of reach. Like many of us, I set goals, achieved them, set new ones, and yet found myself yearning for more. It was not until my forties that I stumbled upon two pivotal truths – well, three if you count the third, which I will share later – that could have saved me decades of misguided steps.

My first truth: Our discontent with something external can stem from an underlying discontent with ourselves. Our perceptions and reactions to external circumstances are often colored by our internal state of being. When we are dissatisfied or unhappy with ourselves, it can manifest as dissatisfaction with various aspects of our lives.

For example, if we are feeling insecure about our abilities, we might find ourselves being overly critical of our work or feeling envious of others' success. If we are struggling with self-worth, we might seek validation and approval from external sources and feel disappointed when it does not come.

Our inner state influences how we perceive the world around us. When we are at peace with ourselves, we are more likely to view external circumstances with clarity and acceptance. Conversely, when we are grappling with internal discontent, we may project those feelings onto our external environment, leading to feelings of dissatisfaction and unrest.

Therefore, addressing our internal state, such as through self-reflection, self-compassion, and personal growth, can often alleviate feelings of discontent with external factors. By silencing the inner critic and nurturing a positive relationship with us, we are better equipped to navigate the challenges and uncertainties of life with greater resilience and peace.

My second truth: Do not shy away from asking questions. As a life coach, I often encourage my clients to question certain aspects of their lives, especially those that may be rooted in limiting beliefs, unhelpful patterns, or assumptions holding them back from realizing their full potential. If certain areas of your life are causing discontent and hindering growth, it might be beneficial to challenge those beliefs, engage in self-reflection, and explore different perspectives.

Pawsitivity Unleashed

By questioning these aspects of your life, you gain clarity on what truly matters to you. This can lead to setting more meaningful goals and aligning them with your values, creating a greater sense of purpose and fulfillment.

However, it is important to balance this with the acceptance of certain things that cannot be changed. As a life coach, having an external guide can help you discern when to let go and when to strive for change, expediting your journey towards transformation. This is why having a personal life coach can be invaluable in the process of growth and change.

As we begin this journey together, I invite you to approach it with an open heart and a curious mind. Alongside sharing my own story and insights, I will provide additional resources and connections to the 30-day journey challenge, offering you tools beyond the workbook journal.

Let us be willing to challenge our current beliefs, be open to exploring new perspectives, and embrace the discomfort that often accompanies growth. It is within this discomfort that the seeds of transformation are planted, ready to blossom into a life of greater meaning and fulfillment.

As you navigate through the book, if you have not yet discovered that one thing that sets your soul on fire, that passion that ignites joy within you every day as it did for me, I hope this tool

Pawsitivity Unleashed

serves as a guide to finding it. I used these very tools to uncover my passion, and it brought immense fulfillment and happiness to my life.

My third truth: Never underestimate the power of even the smallest passions; they often hold the key to the answers we seek. So, as we begin, start aligning your life with things you love and enjoy. Connect with others who share those same passions and make a positive impact with them in some way.

The journey to rediscover, reinvent, and reclaim your life with passion and purpose may not always be easy, but it is undoubtedly the most rewarding. Let us take that first step together.

"Acknowledging the past is not about dwelling on it or getting stuck in it. It is about honoring our journey, recognizing our growth opportunities, and using that awareness to create a brighter and more intentional future."

Kristin Leest

Pawsitivity Unleashed

1

Chapter One

Acknowledging My Beginning

Acknowledging the Past Is the First Step Forward

Growing up in the late '90s amidst my parents' divorce, I witnessed firsthand the immense challenges that single mothers faced. During that time, issues like financial instability, societal judgment, and grueling legal battles shaped the dynamics of our family. Despite the chaos, my mother's unwavering resilience left a profound mark on me. Her strength and determination as she single-handedly led our family empowered me to recognize that I, as the child of one of the strongest women I knew, possessed the same inner strength and capabilities. Witnessing her navigate one of the most pivotal moments of her life, which consequently became one of mine as well, instilled in me the belief that I could conquer any obstacle.

Pawsitivity Unleashed

Throughout those formative years, my mother prepared me to be resilient, to stand tall in the face of adversity, and to understand that even in the darkest moments, I carried within me the strength to persevere. This was a priceless gift that would prove invaluable in the years to come, especially during significant challenges that lay ahead.

In the context of the mid to late '90s, single motherhood carried a significant amount of stigma, although it was not as prevalent or openly discussed as it is today. Many women faced discrimination, which not only impacted their self-esteem but also their sense of belonging in society. Custody battles were emotionally draining, often leaving both mothers and children grappling with the aftermath. Access to essential resources such as healthcare and education was limited, adding to the already substantial burdens these women carried. Financial struggles were commonplace, forcing many to juggle work and parenting responsibilities with little support.

The lack of prevalence of single motherhood during that time also meant that resources and support systems were not as readily available as they are now. Women often had to navigate these challenges on their own, without the extensive network of assistance and understanding that exists today. This made their journey even more arduous and highlighted the remarkable strength and resilience they possessed to overcome such obstacles.

As I reflect on those years and the challenges faced by single mothers like my own, I am reminded of the profound impact they have had on shaping my outlook on life. Their resilience, determination, and unwavering strength serve as a constant inspiration, guiding me to face my own challenges with courage and fortitude. Through those experiences, I have learned invaluable lessons in perseverance, empathy, and the power of unwavering belief in oneself.

Despite the myriad of challenges faced by women as single mothers in the '90s, their resilience and determination shone through. Towards the late '90s and early 2000s, there was a growing recognition of their strength, leading to significant changes in policies and attitudes towards single women.

However, my own experiences during this time as a child witnessing and experiencing the divorce left an indelible mark on me, shifting my focus towards financial security as the number one priority for my future. I was not going to add any burden or struggle to my mother's already full plate, and if I could find a way to free us all financially, I would relieve the stress my father left our family with to solve on our own.

Before my parents' divorce, financial matters had never seemed to be a family concern. We were raised in a wealthy upper-middle-class family, and financial worry did not seem to plague the family ever. My mother was a small business owner, and father a printer.

However, shortly after the divorce, and going from two incomes to one, we had to learn to budget. Our mother always ensured we never went without, but it was not without her or us (meaning myself and my younger sister) having to make many sacrifices. My mother bore the weight alone, continuing to raise her two daughters alone while my father chose to step out and go on his own to start a new life. Over the years, this practice of absent fathers became increasingly common, leaving the women behind to bear the burden of the finances and raising the children alone. It is not to say it does not happen the other way around; however, speaking from a statistical standpoint, 80% of women today in the United States are raising their children alone without their child's father (Census.gov, 2022).

These experiences of uncertainty deeply influenced my decision-making as I entered my early twenties and thirties. I was determined not to burden my mother further, so I approached my career, car, and home choices with caution. Major life decisions loomed larger for me than for many others, bringing on unnecessary stress, anxiety, and fear of failure or inadequacy. I placed this pressure on myself, carrying it with me for years. Our family dynamic had shifted drastically, from a large extended family on my father's side to just my mother, my sister, and me. This change was devastating and traumatic for a woman and two young girls, aged thirteen and eleven at the time, as we had to learn to rely solely on each other.

As this new reality settled in, it became a challenging adjustment emotionally, mentally, and spiritually. However, it also taught me invaluable lessons about resilience, independence, the importance of family and friendship, and the necessity of self-reliance. Reflecting on these pivotal moments, I realized they had a profound impact on many of my subsequent decisions. Over the years, I found myself prioritizing security over pursuing a fulfilling career or taking risks for dream jobs. My priorities became muddled, leading to poor decisions in relationships and opting for safe but less fulfilling life choices. While this approach seemed prudent at the time, it was fueled by fear and the healing process did not occur properly. Consequently, I often felt a nagging sense that something was missing or not right, whether in relationships, jobs, or career paths. It was as if I was chasing my own tail, unable to break free from this cycle.

Fast forward a few years, as a young woman in my late teens and early twenties, I decided to shift my mindset towards what I did not want. It seemed like a straightforward solution — if I could not pinpoint what I desired, I could at least identify what I did not want. So, I began focusing on the negative aspects. However, this approach led to a self-fulfilling prophecy, where my negative thoughts attracted negative outcomes. This marked the beginning

Pawsitivity Unleashed

of what I called the "dark cloud" that followed me everywhere. I realized that what we think or believe can manifest into reality. For instance, completing a task while dwelling only on its negative aspects would inevitably result in a negative experience. This realization aligned with a fundamental principle of personal growth and success known as the Law of Change: when we alter our mindset, our results change accordingly. Our mindset, composed of our beliefs, attitudes, and thoughts, shapes our perceptions, actions, and our outcomes in life.

Consider this: approaching challenges with a negative mindset, convinced of our incapability or impending failure, leads our actions down that path. We may shy away from risks, give up prematurely, or undermine our own efforts, limiting our potential. Conversely, embracing a positive and growth-oriented mindset opens doors to endless possibilities. A growth mindset views challenges as opportunities for growth and learning. Instead of being deterred by setbacks, we see them as steppingstones toward success.

By consciously changing our mindset, we alter our perspective and begin attracting different outcomes. This transformative power lies in understanding that our thoughts and beliefs directly shape the reality we create for ourselves.

Imagine approaching a goal with a mindset of abundance, believing in your capabilities, and viewing setbacks as valuable lessons. With this mindset, you are more likely to persevere through challenges, seek innovative solutions, and achieve success.

The Law of Change reminds us that we have the power to choose our mindset. It is not about ignoring challenges or pretending everything is perfect. Rather, it is about consciously cultivating a mindset that serves our goals and aspirations.

For a long time, fear influenced my decisions, leading me to choose security and safety. It was a protective mechanism, a shield against past experiences. I struggled to discover and embrace my true passion and career path, wandering through various business avenues in search of answers I knew were buried deep within me. I needed to unearth them. Along my journey, I connected with mentors, read self-help books, spoke with therapists from different specialties, and focused on self-discovery, growth, and transformation. It was not until later, with the support of my furry companion, that I began dismantling the walls of negativity, judgment, and fear. Through this process, I finally uncovered my true calling, passion, and purpose. I removed the barriers, used the right tools to find the right answers, and achieved what I had been seeking for so long.

The sense of complete fulfillment I now feel is incredible, content with my life, family, career, and more. Looking back, I wish I had learned these lessons sooner. It would have saved me years of uncertainty and wondering which path to take. That is why I

Pawsitivity Unleashed

created Pawsitivity Unleashed, to share everything I learned over three decades so that others struggling, like I did, would not have to wait as long to find their answers. You can do the work in thirty days and embark on a new journey.

Recently, I celebrated seven years of marriage with my amazing husband. I retired after twenty-one years of military naval service, and together, we raised four beautiful children. I have found success as a wife, mother, entrepreneur, philanthropist, and more.

The most fulfilling part of my journey was discovering my true happiness and purpose, freeing myself from that lingering sense of unfulfillment. Despite the challenges and uncertainties of my past, I emerged stronger, more resilient, and deeply fulfilled. By embracing my true self and conquering my fears, I have built a life that resonates with my values and goals, bringing profound joy to every aspect.

So, as we embark on this 30-day journey together, I invite you to rediscover the profound insights that may lie within you. My goal in sharing my story is to illustrate that success takes many forms, and there is no one-size-fits-all definition. Each person's journey is unique, shaped by individual beliefs, values, and opinions. Success is not solely about wealth; it can be a blend of various elements. By the end of this book, I hope you can define or redefine your idea of success.

Pawsitivity Unleashed

Furthermore, I want to emphasize that even the most successful individuals are just like everyone else. Just as I am like you, and you are like me. If you have picked up this book, it is likely that you, too, are seeking what I once sought - "the answer" to something about yourself that you cannot seem to find on your own. I believe you will discover it here as you undertake the challenge and engage in the discovery work over the thirty-day period.

When starting a journey like this, I prefer to begin from the bottom and work our way up. Let us examine the foundation upon which we are built. What preexisting beliefs might be hindering us? I always recommend reflecting on your childhood to see what you may have brought or carried with you into adulthood. Think back to when you were a young child - who were you? What were your hobbies, your joys? What were your dreams then, and why did they change as you grew older?

As children, we all have dreams of becoming something. Did you achieve that dream? Why or why not? Did someone discourage you from pursuing it? Did you take a different path in life later because someone said the one you were on was not working for you? What obstacles existed in your story? When I did this exercise in my own life, I rediscovered my passion for animals. I found the spark within me that made me excited to wake up and do something meaningful again. I realized I was not satisfied in life because I was not following my heart's true desire. So, I tapped back into that passion, and everything fell into place. I hope that as you do your own exercises, you experience similar "aha" moments. These reflections can lead you to a new beginning, one that inspires and fills your life with fresh excitement and joy.

Our childhood dreams hold the secrets to who we genuinely want to be, free from limitations, fears, or distractions. As we grow older, we often dismiss these dreams as unrealistic. For me, my passion for animals was evident when I was three years old. Every time I revisited happiness, animals were a part of it. I eventually became a dog trainer in 2009, but I still did not pursue it as a full-time career then. I was holding back. Only later, when all the pieces fell into place, did I realize that training added immense value to my life. It not only enriched my skills but also allowed me to add value to those around me. I became more self-reflective, learned to communicate more effectively, and these skills extended beyond dog training into my daily life. That is the power of purpose - it transcends boundaries and enriches every aspect of life.

I encourage you to explore new hobbies during this challenge, as they are also part of the exercises in the workbook. Choose something that has always piqued your interest. If you have a furry companion, consider taking them to a local training class or try an online dog training course. Many references in the book relate to dog training; use it as a tool to train your pup if you wish. Or delve into a different hobby, something you have always wanted to try.

Pawsitivity Unleashed

These lessons are invaluable and will support your journey over the next 30 days.

Remember, success does not happen overnight; it is built over time and with progress. It is an ongoing journey, and you become more successful as you invest more time in yourself. Success is defined by your inner thoughts, emotions, and values, and everyone's definition of success can vary. To achieve success, start by breaking down the walls of prejudice, anger, and resentment. Learn to love and accept yourself, forgive yourself for mistakes and imperfections, and forgive others for their imperfections and wrongdoings. Holding onto negative energy only holds you back from moving forward. Do not let anger or discontent linger, as they only reinforce feelings of insecurity and incompleteness. Instead, win by forgiving, letting go, and moving beyond everything. With a focus on dedication to your growth and a commitment to your well-being, you will find the passion, peace, success, and happiness that led you to this journal and workbook.

If you are ready for a life-changing experience, let us buckle up. The next thirty days are poised to reshape your understanding of yourself. Stick around and let me share my story with you along the way - because together, we are about to begin an incredible journey of rediscovery and purpose, exploring how dog training changed my life. Let us begin!

Pawsitivity Unleashed

2

Chapter Two

Taking On the 30-Day Journey Challenge

What to Expect Over the Next 30 Days

As a successful dog trainer whose love for animals was ignited by the very journey you are about to embark on, I want to express how thrilled I am that you are taking this step. Discovering my true passion and mission allowed me to transform my entire life, turning what could have been seen as a mere hobby into thriving, multi-level businesses. The best part is knowing that I am making a positive impact on both people and animals that matter deeply to me.

In "Pawsitivity Unleashed: Unleashing Life's Lessons, A Journey to Purpose and Passion," I share my personal journey with you and reveal my secrets for success. This revolutionary 30-day challenge is crafted to help you rediscover, reinvent, and reclaim your life through the principles of positive training.

Over the next 30 days, you can dive into this book and complete the daily exercises in the accompanying workbook journal. I highly recommend using both resources, as I provide additional insights and exercises in my memoir that you will find beneficial in your workbook journal. These supplementary exercises can be used to deepen your understanding during the thirty days or to support you on your journey beyond this transformative period.

Within the pages of this book, I share my firsthand experiences, my personal "unraveling," and the path that led me to the same place you are now - seeking to rediscover, reinvent, or reclaim your life. You will resonate with the emotions I experienced throughout my journey, recognizing similar feelings within yourself today. Through my story, you will understand the "catalyst" that sparked my transformation and self-exploration, leading me to build a new foundation for success. All of this is presented as an easy-to-follow daily guide for your 30-day journey ahead.

I have condensed three decades of research and techniques into these daily exercises and activities, providing you with a roadmap for success based on my own journey.

Life Lessons for Days 1-5: Setting the Foundation

Days one through five are dedicated to exploring the foundation of your life. The workbook and journal provide motivational quotes and journaling exercises to stimulate your thoughts and inspire you. The key to initiating change is to begin doing things differently than before. This involves trying new approaches, exploring different ways to accomplish tasks, and considering perspectives you may not have explored previously. Stay open-minded and open-hearted to new adventures, possibilities, and experiences.

In your workbook, the carefully selected daily motivational quotes are intended to spark and fuel your creativity. They will ignite a new innovative idea or invention; the potential is limitless. These quotes are designed to be the catalyst for your journey of self-discovery. Accompanying the quotes are journaling exercises, structured to take between five to fifteen minutes of your time, although you're welcome to invest more time if desired. These exercises act as a tool to unveil your innermost desires, challenges, and aspirations. Through journaling, you can delve into your goals, values, and areas where you might feel stuck. This introspective process serves as the initial step in creating a roadmap for your future.

Importance of Carving Out Time for Yourself

As a mother of four, I understand how finding time for yourself can seem impossible. However, it is essential for your well-being and growth. Even if it is just 15 minutes before the kids wake up or after they have gone to bed, dedicate this time to yourself. Grab a cup of tea, find a quiet space, and read a book or do your journaling exercises. Alternatively, use a portion of a break in the day or any other small window to get time to focus on you. This time is precious—it is your opportunity to focus on your mental health and wellness. As you progress through the month, you will find it easier to prioritize this time as you develop new daily habits and or create a schedule for this is included in your own quiet time.

Building a new Foundation

As we reach Chapter five, you begin embarking on a journey towards setting yourself up for success. This journey involves building upon the foundation you have carefully crafted through your reading, workbook exercises, and journaling revelations. By dedicating regular time for yourself each week and engaging in moments of quiet contemplation and self-reflection, you will notice shifts in your existing foundation. New aspects and qualities of yourself will emerge, signaling the arrival of an updated version of you.

Exercises focused on clarifying values, crafting a vision, nurturing the right mindset, and more will synergize to shape this fresh foundation. Let us investigate these elements and discover how they can spark inspiration within you.

Clarifying Your Values

Here we explore your personal values. Take a moment to identify your top five values and reflect on whether they align with what you initially thought they were. Understanding your core values is crucial when establishing a solid foundation. These values define your identity and principles, acting as a compass that guides your decisions and actions.

We will begin to go deeper into clarifying your core values to ensure they resonate with your vision for your life. When there is a misalignment, it often leads to struggles in various areas such as career choices, life decisions, and overall life satisfaction.

Creating a Vision and Setting Goals

Once you have a clear picture of your core values, we can start envisioning the life you want by creating a map of exactly the life you want and how to get it. We will work on setting meaningful, inspiring goals that align with these values. These goals will serve as your roadmap, guiding your actions and keeping you focused on what truly matters to you.

Pawsitivity Unleashed

Establishing Mindset Shifts

Here we learn about the importance of mindset and mindset shifts. Our mindset shapes our reality. Often, we do not realize the number of negative thoughts we tell ourselves or that are brought to our attention daily. If we can change the way we look at the world around us, we can reshape our mindset and watch it shift in a positive direction. We will learn how to focus on cultivating a positive and growth-oriented mindset. This involves challenging limiting beliefs and negative thought patterns that have been holding us back for so long. Then we look at replacing them with empowering thoughts and beliefs. This will begin to open doors and remove the barriers that limit your current situation and move you on to the next step toward a more fulfilling and rewarding life and more.

The Importance of Self-Care and Overall Well-Being

Here we learn and emphasize that your health and well-being should never be compromised. Self-care is non-negotiable. We will highlight the critical importance of self-care, encompassing physical, mental, and emotional health.

We discuss the significance of integrating small self-care activities into your daily schedule to cultivate mindfulness. These practices can include regular exercise, nourishing foods, and adequate rest. By prioritizing these elements, you will enhance your overall well-being and begin to feel better from the inside out.

Embracing Personal Growth

In our fast-paced lives, it is easy to lose sight of ourselves and prioritize others' needs over our own. This includes neglecting our own personal development. Committing to lifelong learning and growth is crucial for ongoing fulfillment, happiness, and success.

In this section we learn how personal development manifests in various forms. We explore avenues for personal growth, be it through books, courses, workshops, or coaching. Continuously expanding your knowledge and skills unlocks new possibilities and fosters personal growth. It sharpens your mind and keeps your brain constantly engaged in learning.

Setting Boundaries and Building up Self-Respect

Another vital aspect of your journey toward rediscovery is the examination of boundaries and self-respect. Achieving success involves learning how to establish healthy boundaries. Prior to this step, we might struggle with the inability to say no to things that do not align with our values or well-being. If you find yourself dissatisfied in this area of your life, it could be because you are not expressing your feelings and opinions when asked to share them. By prioritizing self-respect and honoring your needs, you will lay a solid foundation for healthy relationships. As a result, the quality of your relationships will begin to elevate, better meeting your needs.

Building Supportive Relationships

Having supportive relationships is essential for everyone, yet many struggle to build them or find the right people to lean on when needed. Surrounding yourself with positive and supportive individuals is invaluable, and it begins with knowing how to support yourself and provide what you need during challenging times. Once you have mastered self-support, you can then learn to express these needs to those closest to you.

In our discussions, we emphasize the significance of cultivating deep and meaningful connections with friends, family, mentors, and like-minded individuals. We explore how to initiate and nurture these relationships. They will serve as a dedicated support system throughout your journey, acting as sounding boards and providing support when faced with challenges.

Creating Financial Health

Finances are a crucial aspect of our lives. Financial stress can be overwhelming, especially if we have never had the luxury or support of receiving quality financial advice or guidance. This burden can significantly impact our financial health. That is why we will emphasize the importance of taking charge of your financial well-being by creating a budget, saving wisely, and planning.

Financial stability not only provides a sense of security but also the freedom to pursue your passions. With a solid financial foundation, you can reduce stress and worry, allowing yourself the liberty to try new experiences and embark on exciting ventures.

The Importance of Gratitude Practice Daily

An essential part of rediscovering, reinventing, or reclaiming your life is cultivating gratitude for your past, the journey you have taken, and the people who supported you along the way. Gratitude is a potent tool for nurturing a positive mindset. As part of our process, we will integrate a regular gratitude practice into your routine.

Through expressing gratitude for even the smallest blessings, you will shift your focus from scarcity to abundance. This simple yet profound act can transform your perspective and help you appreciate the richness of your life's experiences.

The Importance of Acting and Accountability

To wrap up, I want to stress the significance of taking consistent action towards your goals. Together, we will break down your goals into manageable steps and craft a solid plan of action.

Holding yourself accountable and celebrating your progress will keep you motivated and focused.

By setting a strong foundation rooted in your values, vision, mindset, self-care, boundaries, relationships, finances, gratitude, and action, you are paving the way for a fulfilling and purposeful life. Each step we take together on this journey will bring you closer to the life you envision.

Life Lessons for Days 6-10: Cultivating Pawsitivity

Days six through ten of your journeys are dedicated to cultivating "pawsitivity" in your thoughts, actions, and relationships. This phase is crucial for continuing to build a solid foundation on your 30-day path of rediscovery, reinvention, and reclaiming your life. Leveraging my experiences as a dog trainer, I share insights on patience, consistency, and compassion, providing daily exercises that promote gratitude, mindfulness, and self-care. These exercises are crafted to nurture an abundance mindset, a vital component of fostering pawsitivity on your transformative journey.

What is Pawsitivity?

"Pawsitivity" is not just a principle in dog training; it is a philosophy that extends into your 30-day journey. It transcends mere positivity; it is a mindset that influences every aspect of your life,

Pawsitivity Unleashed

shaping how you tackle challenges, navigate relationships, and seize opportunities. Cultivating pawsitivity opens the doors to a realm of possibilities and potential for personal growth. I have applied this concept in training dogs, with my coaching clients, and now you too can apply it to your own life. Through daily practice and analysis, you will learn how to cultivate this mindset and integrate it into your daily routines.

How Do You Cultivate Pawsitivity?

Step 1: Create Awareness of Thoughts and Emotions. Start by being mindful of your thoughts and emotions. When negative thoughts arise, make a conscious effort to shift them towards more positive ones. View challenges as opportunities for personal growth, focus on gratitude, and actively seek out the positive in every situation.

Step 2: Begin Practicing Gratitude. Set aside time each day to reflect on the things you are thankful for, no matter how small they may seem. This practice can help shift your perspective and allow you to see the abundance in your life, fostering a sense of contentment and appreciation.

Step 3: Begin Practicing Self-Compassion. Treat yourself with kindness and understanding, especially during moments of mistakes or setbacks. Embrace your humanity and allow yourself moments of struggle. Practicing self-compassion builds resilience and inner strength.

Step 4: Create Positive Influences. Surround yourself with positive influences by seeking out uplifting and supportive relationships. Spend time with friends who inspire you, join communities of like-minded you, or work with a coach or mentor who believes in your potential.

Step 5: Participate in Joyful Activities. Be available for activities that bring you joy and fulfillment. Whether it is pursuing a hobby, spending time in nature, or practicing mindfulness, these activities nourish your soul and elevate your mood. Prioritizing joyful experiences enhances your overall well-being and contributes to a more positive mindset.

What is the Ripple Effect When It Comes to Pawsitivity?

As you embark on the journey of creating and nurturing pawsitivity in your daily life, you will begin to witness what I like to call "the ripple effect" in various facets of your life. This ripple effect manifests as improvements in your relationships, the emergence of new opportunities, and increased resilience in the face of challenges. It all starts when you consciously make choices each day to cultivate a positive and empowered mindset.

Pawsitivity Unleashed

Imagine this ripple effect as dropping a pebble into a still pond. The initial action of dropping the pebble represents your commitment to pawsitivity. As the ripples spread outward, they touch every aspect of your life. Your interactions with others become more harmonious and supportive as you radiate positivity. The doors of opportunity swing open as your mindset shifts from limitation to possibility. Even when faced with obstacles, you find yourself equipped with the inner strength and resilience to overcome them.

However, it is crucial to understand that cultivating pawsitivity is not a one-time task but an ongoing, daily practice. It is about approaching each day with mindfulness and intention, making choices that align with your values and aspirations. By consistently applying these principles, you will not only experience the benefits in your own life but also create a ripple effect that positively impacts those around you.

Life Lessons for Days 11-15: Unleashing Potential

In the next phase of your 30-day journey, spanning from days eleven to fifteen, we discuss the exciting territory of unleashing your potential. This phase is dedicated to helping you maintain consistency in the new healthy habits you have cultivated, such as journaling and self-reflection. It is all about empowering yourself to embrace change rather than fear or avoid it.

Pawsitivity Unleashed

During these days, we focus on strategies and action plans to overcome obstacles that may arise along the way. The workbook becomes a valuable tool as we dive into visualization techniques, goal setting exercises, and harnessing the power of intention to manifest the life you desire.

Embracing change can be a powerful catalyst for growth and transformation. By shifting your mindset from one of resistance to one of openness, you open the door to endless possibilities. We will explore how to approach change with curiosity and excitement, seeing it as an opportunity for personal evolution rather than a threat.

Through the exercises and reflections in the workbook, you will gain clarity on your goals and aspirations. You will learn how to create actionable steps towards these goals, breaking them down into manageable tasks. Visualization techniques will help you see yourself achieving these goals, making them feel more attainable and real.

This phase is all about stepping into your potential and embracing the journey of growth. It is about taking intentional steps towards the life you envision for yourself, with confidence and determination. As you work through these lessons, remember that change is not something to be feared but embraced as a powerful force for personal development and fulfillment.

Pawsitivity Unleashed

Unleashing Your Potential

Unleashing your potential is akin to discovering a hidden treasure within yourself – a journey of tapping into the limitless possibilities that lie dormant within and bringing them to light. As your dedicated life coach, I am here to be your guide on this transformative path of self-discovery and growth.

Key Steps to Unleash Potential and Lead You to Success:

Step 1: Believe in Yourself. The foundation of unleashing your potential begins with unwavering self-belief. Cultivate a mindset of confidence, positivity, and self-assurance. Recognize and honor the unique strengths, talents, and gifts that reside within you, waiting to be shared with the world.

Step 2: Clarify Your Vision. Envision your ideal life – what does it look like? What are your deepest passions and dreams? Set clear, inspiring goals that serve as a roadmap toward unlocking your potential. Break these goals down into actionable steps, creating a tangible path forward.

Step 3: Take Consistent Action. Every step, no matter how small, moves you closer to realizing your full potential. Stay focused, committed, and persistent, especially in the face of challenges. Consistent action is the key to progress and growth.

Step 4: Embrace Growth. Embrace a mindset of continuous learning and openness to new experiences. Step out of your comfort zone and expand your horizons. Growth and transformation flourish when you embrace challenges as opportunities for development.

Step 5: Build a Supportive Community. Surround yourself with a supportive community of like-minded you who uplift and inspire you. Seek out mentors, coaches, or friends who believe in your potential and encourage you to reach higher.

Step 6: Prioritize Self-Care. Nourish your mind, body, and spirit through dedicated self-care practices. Whether it is meditation, exercise, journaling, or spending time in nature, prioritize activities that replenish and energize you for the journey ahead.

Step 7: Celebrate Successes. Acknowledge and celebrate every success, no matter how small. Recognizing your progress fuels motivation and momentum, propelling you forward toward your goals with renewed vigor.

By following these steps, you will be well on your way to unleashing the full extent of your potential and creating a life filled with purpose, fulfillment, and success. Together, let us embark on this empowering journey of self-discovery and growth.

The Importance of Embracing Your Journey

Keep in mind that unleashing your potential is a continuous journey of growth, discovery, and self-mastery, so remember to fully embrace every moment of your path. It is all about embracing your authentic self and boldly stepping into your greatness with courage and confidence. Every step you take forward is a step closer to unlocking the remarkable potential that lies within you.

Life Lessons for Days 16-20: Embracing Change

During days sixteen through twenty, we continue to explore the theme of embracing change, a crucial aspect of the journey of self-discovery. This phase delves deeper into the process of adapting to change, navigating challenges, and cultivating resilience through engaging workbook exercises. Furthermore, we highlight the importance of celebrating progress and staying focused on your goals.

The Importance of Embracing Change

Embracing change can present a formidable challenge for anyone. It often means stepping out of our comfort zones, a task that can feel daunting. Like many of you, I faced difficulties when change was necessary. We become accustomed to our routines, even when they no longer benefit us. This familiarity offers a sense of security, but it can also lead to stagnation, unfulfillment, or discomfort.

Navigating Your Journey Successfully

As you progress through the thirty-day challenge, it is important to acknowledge any discomfort you may feel. These moments of discomfort present some of the biggest opportunities for change. Feeling apprehensive, anxious, or resistant to change is completely normal. These emotions are natural responses to the unknown. However, it is crucial to take small, deliberate steps forward even when the changes seem uncertain or frightening.

Learning to Clarify Your Goals

To navigate your journey effectively, it is crucial to clarify your goals. Whether you write them down, keep a separate list, or track them, staying organized will help you reach your ultimate objectives. Take some time to delve into the reasons behind your desire for change. What do you hope to achieve? What positive outcomes do you envision once this change is realized? By clarifying your goals and motivations, you create a roadmap for yourself, guiding your path toward transformation.

Making Incremental Progress, Is Progress

Recognizing the value of incremental progress is essential. By breaking down changes into manageable steps, the entire process becomes less daunting. Rather than aiming for a complete overhaul, focus on small, incremental changes that can easily fit into your daily routine. Each small achievement serves as a sign of progress and should be acknowledged and celebrated along the way.

How to Navigate Setbacks

It is important to keep in mind that this journey is just that—a journey. Like any journey, there will be setbacks and bumps along the road. Change does not always follow a straight path; it is more like a series of difficulties. During these setbacks and moments of doubt, it is crucial to cultivate self-compassion. Treat yourself with the same kindness and understanding that you would offer to a close friend going through a similar challenge. Remember that setbacks are not failures; they are opportunities for learning and growth.

How to Build the Right Support

Finally, building a support system for those moments when things feel too overwhelming to tackle alone will be crucial. Making changes and breaking old habits takes time and effort. Surround yourself with a supportive network of friends, family, or even a therapist. Having this support system can provide encouragement, accountability, and guidance as you navigate the path of change. Sharing your journey with others can also alleviate the sense of isolation and offer valuable perspectives.

As we continue to review the theme of embracing change, it is important to remember that transformation is a gradual process that unfolds over time. Stay committed to your goals and remember to celebrate even the smallest victories along the way. Each step forward, no matter how small, is a step toward realizing your full potential. Together, we will navigate this journey with resilience and determination, knowing that growth and self-discovery await us at every turn.

Life Lessons for Days 21-25: Reinventing Yourself

Days twenty-one to twenty-five of your journey focus on the theme of reinventing yourself. This phase offers opportunities to explore new possibilities and passions, igniting your creativity and imagination. As a life coach, I have witnessed incredible transformations in those who have dared to reinvent themselves. It is about stepping into the unknown with courage and openness, allowing yourself to explore new horizons and passions.

Embracing All the Possibilities

Embrace possibility. Do not get caught up in what others might think or say. Reinvention starts by shedding limiting beliefs and adopting a mindset of possibility. We often cling to outdated ideas about ourselves based on past experiences or societal norms. However, the process of reinvention challenges us to question these beliefs and envision ourselves in fresh and exciting ways.

Taking Part in Creative Exploration

Let your creativity flow! Creative exercises are essential on this journey as they act as powerful tools to tap into your imagination and discover potential that may have been lying dormant within you. Whether it is through journaling, creating vision boards, or engaging in artistic expression, these exercises help you visualize the life you desire and chart a course to reach it.

Dare to Dream and Dream Big!

Embrace the power of "dreaming big." You heard this phrase as a child, maybe not as an adult, but I am here to remind you of its importance. It is your turn now. Take a moment to dare to dream, and when you do, dream big! This is your opportunity to envision the life you've always desired. Allow yourself to fully immerse yourself in this vision. Give yourself permission to dream of a life that genuinely excites and inspires you. Ask yourself: What are my passions? What activities bring me joy and fulfillment? By exploring these questions, you uncover hidden talents and interests that have been waiting to be explored.

Taking Purposeful Action in your journey

Take decisive action with the decisions you make towards the life you want to reinvent or lead going forward. Formulate a plan, and ensure each step is purposeful and meaningful. Reinvention requires taking tangible steps forward. It is about stepping beyond your comfort zone and pursuing your passions with intent. This may involve exploring new experiences, enrolling in classes, or connecting with individuals who share your interests and aspirations.

Integrating Past Experiences into your Present and Future

We all have learned valuable lessons from our experiences. They have led us to this very moment today. Integrate your past experiences into your present and your future. Give meaning and value to what you have endured or overcome. It is crucial to understand that reinvention does not mean discarding your past entirely. Instead, it is about integrating all that you have learned and experienced into this new chapter of your life. Your past experiences have shaped you, and now you can use them as steppingstones toward your reinvented self.

Navigating the Process with Strategy

Navigate the process with strategy and thought. As you embark on this journey of reinvention, remember that it is a process. There may be moments of uncertainty or fear, and that is perfectly normal. Trust in your inner wisdom and the guidance provided in the workbook. Each step you take brings you closer to the vibrant, reinvented version of yourself that you are striving to become.

Reinvention is a bold and transformative journey, one that requires courage, creativity, and openness to new possibilities. By daring to dream big, embracing change, and taking purposeful action, you are laying the foundation for a life that truly reflects your passions and aspirations.

Life Lessons for Days 26-30: Reclaiming Your Life

Days twenty-six to thirty are dedicated to the powerful theme of reclaiming your life and stepping into your power. This phase of your journey is about taking bold action aligned with your values and creating a roadmap for sustainable success and fulfillment. As your life coach, I am here to support you every step of the way as you embark on this transformative path.

Focusing on Self-Discovery and Reflection

Self-discovery and reflection will be pivotal as you reclaim your life as your own. It is about diving deep into who you are and what truly matters to you. Take time to explore your past experiences, both positive and negative, and how they have shaped you. Identify the patterns or beliefs that have been holding you back and gain clarity on where you stand.

Empowering Yourself with Goal Setting

Empower yourself by setting goals that align with your values and passions. These goals should be SMART: Specific, Measurable, Achievable, Relevant, and Time-bound. They will serve as guiding lights on your path toward a life that feels authentic and fulfilling.

Letting Go of the Old

Let go of the old and recreate and shape the newest version of you. Reclaiming your life involves letting go of what no longer serves you. This might include toxic relationships, self-limiting beliefs, or habits that hold you back. By releasing these burdens, you create space for new opportunities and growth.

Creating a Supportive Community

Continue to grow your supportive community. Surround yourself with supportive friends, family, or a coach who believes in your potential. Having accountability and encouragement from others can be a powerful force in reclaiming your life. Share your goals and aspirations with those who uplift and inspire you.

Continuing to Practice Self-Care and Self-Love

Continue to practice self-care and self-love. Throughout this journey, prioritizing self-care and self-love is necessary. It is often the first thing we stop doing for ourselves when we get stressed and over busy, but we need new routines. Nurture your mind, body, and spirit through activities that bring you joy and peace. Whether it is through meditation, yoga, spending time in nature, or pursuing a beloved hobby, these practices will replenish your energy and keep you grounded.

Learning to Embrace Your Authenticity

Embrace your authenticity. You will begin to see the real parts of you shine through again, and those are the parts of your authentic self you do not want to lose again. Reclaiming your life is about stepping into your authenticity fully. Embrace who you truly are, unapologetically. This means honoring your values, passions, and unique qualities. When you live authentically, you align with your true essence and create a life that reflects your deepest desires.

Celebrating Progress Along the Way

Continue to celebrate your progress. As you continue your journey here, it will be essential for you to celebrate every step of the way. It is empowering and motivating as you begin to see changes and do not see changes but are making progress. Set goals and make plans to celebrate regardless of how small it may seem and honor your victories. Each milestone reached is a testament to your inner strength and unwavering determination.

Reclaiming your life is a profound and deeply rewarding journey. It is one of the biggest gifts you can give yourself. The process is about taking full ownership of your story, embracing your inherent power, and crafting a life that resonates with the depths of your soul.

This 30-Day Journey serves as your transformative roadmap. Through poignant quotes, introspective journaling exercises, and engaging activities, you begin to embark on a path of self-discovery guided by the principles of pawsitive training I have used for over fourteen years. By embracing these principles and taking intentional, inspired action, you will unlock your true potential like I did with a life filled with purpose, meaning, and unbridled joy.

My first gift and #1 Secret to ensure you have a successful journey, begins with creating consistency in everything you do. Why is consistency so crucial? Consistency is the key to building momentum

Pawsitivity Unleashed

and progress. When you are consistent, you develop strong habits that propel you forward towards your goals. It is not just about what you do during the journey but also about what you continue to do afterward. Here's why consistency matters:

1. Building Momentum:

Consistency builds momentum. Each small action you take consistently adds up over time, creating a snowball effect of progress. It is like pushing a heavy rock uphill; at first, it might feel slow and challenging, but as you keep pushing consistently, it becomes easier and gains momentum.

2. Developing Strong Habits:

Consistency helps you develop strong, positive habits. When you consistently engage in certain behaviors, they become ingrained in your routine. These habits become second nature, making it easier for you to stay on track even when faced with challenges.

3. Sustaining Progress:

By creating consistency, you ensure that the progress you make during your journey does not fade away once the journey is over. The habits you establish during this time can continue to serve you long after the journey ends, leading to sustained success and fulfillment.

4. Building Trust and Confidence:

Consistency builds trust and confidence in yourself. When you consistently show up for yourself and follow through with your commitments, you strengthen your belief in your abilities. This confidence propels you forward and fuels further success.

5. Overcoming Resistance:

Consistency helps you overcome resistance and obstacles. There will be times when you face challenges or feel demotivated. Consistency acts as a buffer during these times, providing you with a solid foundation to keep moving forward.

6. Creating Lasting Change:

Consistency is the bridge between setting goals and achieving them. It is the driving force behind lasting change. When you consistently work towards your goals, you are more likely to achieve them and maintain the results over time.

Consistency is the secret ingredient that turns dreams into reality. It transforms effort into habit, obstacles into opportunities, and intentions into actions. So, focus on remaining consistent throughout your journey and beyond. Build those strong habits, stay committed, and watch as your efforts yield lasting and meaningful results.

Envision yourself and your faithful furry companion navigating life's unpredictable twists and turns together. This embodies "The Power of Pawsitive." Just like in the world of sports or dog training, consistency is the secret sauce to success. During my high school varsity softball years, the importance of consistency was deeply ingrained in me from the very start. If you have played sports or any competitive team activity, this should resonate with you.

Starting as a pitcher at just thirteen years old, I was already playing catch-up. Girls had been involved in softball for the last six years, so I had much ground to cover if I wanted to compete. This was no small challenge, but my unwavering determination pushed me forward. I practiced tirelessly, surrounded by a supportive community of family, friends, coaches, and other passionate girls that fueled my ambition.

Consistency was crucial to bridge the gap. Qualifying for an elite travel team that practiced year-round was a significant change. This granted me more playing time and access to indoor facilities for pitching, training, and batting regularly. Consistent training was pivotal. It distinguished me from the other girls in the league who only practiced when the season began. It became the corner-stone of my success. Girls in California, on these travel leagues,

Pawsitivity Unleashed

have the advantage of year-round practice due to their favorable weather, a benefit not mirrored on the East Coast. However, this did not discourage me. We would face those teams later in the summer championship; as I prepared, fear did not deter my readiness.

I committed to daily practices, and it generated a powerful momentum for me. This led to becoming the starting pitcher in the middle school leagues and gaining recognition as an upcoming star in local newspapers. I continued to establish positive, consistent habits, laying the solid foundation for the lasting transformation we will delve into later. I showed up for myself each day at every practice, whether sore, tired, or just not feeling up to it. It was precisely during challenges or moments of doubt when genuine progress unfolded, and I pushed through. Learning new pitches, throwing harder, and honing my skills. At the age of fourteen, reaching sixty miles an hour was significant, especially during the nineties. It took about a year of dedication to unlock the extent of my hidden potential, but I was determined to continue growing even more. As we learn, success comes when we meet and achieve goals, but it is all cyclical and continuous. We need to pace ourselves and focus on the main objective, celebrating all the small wins along the way.

Consistency, dedication, and support collectively brought me success in the game of softball. Just as with dog training, success comes when a dog consistently masters commands, and the trainer reinforces desired behaviors with proper techniques while building a strong bond with their client or dog. You can apply these same principles to other aspects of your life – whether rediscovering, re-inventing, or reclaiming yourself, the process is similar. You start with simple yet impactful practices like gratitude journaling, mindful meditation, or regular exercise and create new consistent habits that incorporate these tasks into your daily life. The self-reflection and inspiration from these tasks act as your catalyst for change, leading you to newfound success in personal growth and meeting the life goals you set to achieve.

As you steadfastly commit to these daily practices, you will witness small shifts in your life. Profound connections in the principles of pawsitive training, which we will explore shortly, will become apparent in your journey. We learned earlier that cultivating a pawsitive mindset has the potential to transform every aspect of your life, and it truly does. It is a fundamental cornerstone for personal development. So, as you begin to work through the daily practices in your workbook and journal, remain committed to your goal. Your passion and diligence will naturally radiate pawsitivity to others during your process of change. Together, we will unlock your boundless potential and create lives filled with purpose, fulfillment, and unbridled joy. Making every day count will become effortless.

In our modern, fast-paced world, many of us grapple with feelings of disconnection, overwhelm, and a persistent sense of

Pawsitivity Unleashed

unfulfillment. We all yearn for a sense of purpose and the passion that accompanies it. When life takes us far off the beaten path, we long for someone to jumpstart our lives and guide us back to that feeling of completeness, wholeness, and passion. Often, when we stray, we do not know how we got there or how to rekindle that spark of inspiration. However, you now hold all the answers. Let us embark on this journey together!

3

Chapter Three

Applying the Principles of Pawsitive Living

What are the Principles of Pawsitive Living

In the previous chapter, I introduced the concept of principles of "Pawsitive Training." These principles were the foundation around my dog training sessions for fourteen years. Over the years, what became evident was that those very same principles also helped my owners to connect with their furry companion and to me as their trainer. It was clear there was extreme value in these principles and that they could not only benefit dogs and their owners' relationships but the owner's relationship and how they relate to the world. The parallels between dog training and self-improvement skills were strikingly similar. I began implementing the principles in my own life and that is how what we know as the principles of

Pawsitivity Unleashed

pawsitive training skills became the Principles of Pawsitive Living that I now use with my life coaching clients. These principles, serve as a roadmap to create and establish a balance in the life of whomever you work with, while offering anyone using the tools the opportunity to receive and achieve greater fulfillment and meaning in their lives just buy implementing the principles.

This invaluable tool acts as an excellent resource and reference in my own life, especially during challenging times. When I was faced with challenges I could not solve on my own or could not find the answers I was seeking, I turned to the principles. I would go through each one and ask myself if I was actively implementing each principle. If I were not, I would make the change and see if I were able to solve my problem or issue. If it did not, I moved on to the next principle. I applied each principle until I was able to come to the answer of my own challenge. It worked every time. They served as a guiding light when I needed additional support. A third-party perspective without an opinion, just perspective. It was everything I needed.

I learned that the principles enhanced my abilities to nurture qualities of resilience, compassion, effective communication, and a positive mindset. These attributes not only enhanced my life, but my skills as a trainer, a parent, mother, friend, and I saw positive changes within the people I surrounded myself with.

Whether you have your own furry companion that you work with and train, have your own dog training business or are seeking a

Pawsitivity Unleashed

personal transformation in your own life, these principles of pawsitive living, can support you on any life journey goal with proven success. I have personally used them to navigate my own journey and used them in countless life coach transformations that helped people just like you and me reshape their lives to meet their individual desired goals.

As you review each principle you will see principles that quality dog trainers have used for years in their own programs for decades and proved effective. Professional coaches in the field of life coaching use these same skills with phenomenal results, but before we discuss the top one hundred principles of pawsitive living, it is crucial to understand the foundational principles necessary to create a lasting transformation. These principles serve as the bedrock upon which we build a successful transformation.

4 Key Pawsitive Principles to a Lasting Transformation

As a dog trainer, I have witnessed firsthand the transformative power of the pawsitive principles. Not only in the lives of our furry friends but also in their human companions. Pawsitive living is not just a catchy phrase; it is a way of life that can bring about profound changes in our mindset, behavior, and overall well-being.

Pawsitive living revolves around fostering a mindset of optimism, gratitude, and kindness. It is about approaching life's challenges with a can-do attitude, focusing on solutions rather than dwelling on problems. Just as when I train dogs to respond to positive reinforcement, we too can train our own minds to see the good in every situation and respond with grace and positivity.

The first pawsitive principle necessary to create a lasting transformation is gratitude. Gratitude is a powerful force that can shift our perspective from lack to abundance. When we cultivate a mindset of gratitude, we train ourselves to see the blessings in our lives, no matter how small they may seem. This principle is closely tied to the concept of living in the moment, a trait often exemplified by our canine companions.

Dogs are experts at living in the present moment. They do not dwell on the past or worry about the future; they simply enjoy the here and now. As their human counterparts, we can learn a valuable lesson from this. By practicing mindfulness and being fully present in each moment, we can savor life's simple pleasures and find joy in the little things.

The second essential pawsitive principle is kindness. Dogs are naturally compassionate creatures, offering unconditional love and support to those around them. They do not judge or hold grudges; they simply offer love and acceptance. As humans, we can strive to emulate this behavior by showing kindness and compassion to ourselves and others.

Kindness extends not only to those we interact with but also to ourselves. Self-compassion is a crucial aspect of pawsitive living. Just as I encourage my dog owners to be patient and gentle with their dogs during training, we must also extend that same kindness to ourselves. We are so often our own harshest critics, but by practicing self-compassion, we can cultivate inner peace and acceptance.

The third essential pawsitive principle is optimism Another cornerstone to pawsitive living. Dogs approach each day with a sense of optimism and enthusiasm, eager to explore and experience new adventures. While life may throw us curveballs, maintaining a hopeful outlook can help us navigate challenges with resilience and grace.

As a dog trainer and life coach, I have witnessed firsthand how embracing these principles can lead to a lasting transformation. After completing my 30-day journey to reinvent, rediscover and reclaim your life with purpose and passion and applying the principles of pawsitive living, your journey after just becomes a way of life — a new guiding philosophy that shapes your thoughts, actions, and interactions.

But how would you continue to embrace pawsitive living beyond the thirty-day challenge?

It begins with remaining consistent with your skills and techniques you learn from this book and the workbook/journal and practicing mindfulness. Just as we reinforce desired behaviors in dogs through

Pawsitivity Unleashed

consistent training, we must also reinforce pawsitive habits in ourselves. This might include daily practices of gratitude journaling which helps cultivate a mindset of abundance and appreciation. Or daily practice and use of affirmations. Both practices have profound effects on our overall outlook on life.

Lastly, another powerful and essential principle is mindfulness. By practicing mindfulness, we learn to observe our thoughts and emotions without judgment, allowing us to respond to situations with clarity and composure. This practice not only reduces stress and anxiety but also helps us stay grounded in the present moment.

Performing acts of kindness, no matter how small, is also great and plays a crucial role in maintaining a pawsitive mindset. Whether it is offering a helping hand to a neighbor or simply smiling at a stranger, these acts of kindness not only brighten someone else's day but also fill our own hearts with warmth and joy.

We mentioned affirmation above but focusing on optimism through positive affirmations and visualization as we mentioned before is equally important. By repeating affirmations such as "I am capable," "I am worthy," and "I am resilient," allows us to we rewire our brains to focus on the positive aspects of ourselves and our lives. Visualization techniques, where we imagine ourselves achieving our goals and living our best lives, also help bolster optimism and motivation.

Incorporating these practices into our daily lives allows us to stay true to the pawsitive principles that guide us. It is important to remember that pawsitive living is not about perfection; it is about progress. There will be days when we falter, when negativity creeps in, but it is how we respond to these moments that truly matters.

As you continue your journey to pawsitive living, focus on surrounding yourself with a supportive community. Just as dogs thrive in a loving and nurturing environment, we flourish too when surrounded by like-minded individuals like yourself that can lift you up and inspire you. Whether it is joining a meditation group, attending pawsitive living workshops, or simply connecting with friends who share your values, community support is essential for maintaining a pawsitive mindset.

Living a pawsitive life is not just about following a set of principles; it is about embodying a mindset of optimism, gratitude, kindness, and resilience. I have seen firsthand the profound impact that embracing pawsitive living can have. After your thirty-day challenge journey you have created new good healthy pawsitive habits that incorporate pawsitive living- continuing those habits should become a way of life for you —a guiding philosophy that shapes your thoughts, actions, and interactions.

In time, you will find yourself cultivating gratitude, mindfulness, kindness, and optimism, creating a ripple effect of positivity that

Pawsitivity Unleashed

transforms not only your life but also touches the lives of those around you.

Here is the complete list of the one hundred principles of pawsitive living. Take a moment to review them and let them serve as a reminder to embrace life with enthusiasm, just as a dog wags its tail with joy. Whether in training or in life, these principles are not just suggested; they are essential and are the core to your transformation that lies ahead.

The One Hundred Principles to Pawsitive Living

1. Start with a Wag: Approach each day with a positive attitude.
2. See the Tail Wag: Look for good in every situation.
3. Embrace the Learning Curve: Every experience is an opportunity to gain experience.
4. Paws for Reflection: Take time to reflect on experiences.
5. Tailor Your Approach: Adapt your approach to situations.
6. Stay Pawsitive: Maintain a positive outlook.
7. Treat Life as a Training Session: See challenges as opportunities.
8. Celebrate Small Victories: Acknowledge every success.
9. Trust the Process: Believe in the process of growth.
10. Embrace Imperfection: Focus on progress, not perfection.
11. Practice Gratitude: Be thankful for the positives.
12. Focus on Solutions, Not Problems: Troubleshoot challenges.
13. Welcome New Tricks: Be open to learning.
14. Tailor Your Treats: Reward yourself appropriately.
15. Consistent Kindness: Approach interactions with kindness.
16. Live in the Moment: Embrace the present.
17. Training Takes Time: Be patient with progress.
18. Redirect, Don't Punish: Focus on positive actions.
19. Reward Effort: Acknowledge challenging work.
20. Cultivate Curiosity: Stay open-minded.
21. Listen with Your "Dog Ears": Truly listen to others.

Pawsitivity Unleashed

22. Use Your Non-Verbal "Tail Wag": Positive body language is key.

23. Communicate Clearly: Be direct and honest.

24. Use Positive Reinforcement: Encourage good behavior.

25. Be an Active Listener: Engage fully in conversations.

26. Speak Kindly: Use gentle words.

27. Teach by Example: Lead with your actions.

28. Tailor Your "Commands": Adjust communication styles.

29. Create a Safe Space: Foster a safe environment.

30. Show Affection: Offer genuine love and appreciation.

31. Use Positive Words: Speak positively.

32. Empathize with Others: Understand their perspective.

33. Teach, Don't Preach: Share knowledge inspiringly.

34. Stay Present in Conversations: Give full attention.

35. Find Common Ground: Build connections.

36. Acknowledge Others' Strengths: Appreciate talents.

37. Offer Encouragement: Support others.

38. Stay Calm in Conflict: Handle conflicts calmly.

39. Apologize When Necessary: Be humble and apologize.

40. Foster Trust: Build trust through honesty.

41. Stay Playful: Keep a playful spirit.

42. Seek Feedback: Learn from feedback.

43. Challenge Yourself: Push beyond comfort zones.

44. Adapt and Evolve: Adjust to change.

45. Invest in Learning: Never stop growing.

46. Set "Training" Goals: Define clear objectives.

Pawsitivity Unleashed

47. Embrace Diversity: Celebrate differences.

48. Practice Self-Compassion: Be kind to yourself.

49. Stay Persistent: Keep going despite challenges.

50. Visualize Success: Imagine achieving goals.

51. Take Breaks: Rest and recharge.

52. Stay Healthy: Prioritize well-being.

53. Learn from Failure: See failure as a lesson.

54. Practice Mindfulness: Stay present.

55. Stay Flexible: Adapt to changes.

56. Cultivate Resilience: Bounce back from setbacks.

57. Visualize Positivity: Focus on positive outcomes.

58. Celebrate Self-Improvement: Acknowledge growth.

59. Stay Grounded: Remain humble.

60. Stay Inspired: Seek inspiration.

61. Build a Support System: Surround yourself with a supportive community.

62. Give Back: Contribute positively.

63. Share Your "Toys": Be generous with resources.

64. Forgive and Forget: Let go of grudges.

65. Create a "Pack" Mentality: Foster unity in relationships.

66. Be Loyal: Stand by loved ones.

67. Celebrate Others' Success: Cheer for others' achievements.

68. Offer a Helping Paw: Support those in need.

69. Practice Inclusion: Include everyone.

70. Stay Playful in Relationships: Keep interactions fun.

71. Be a Good Listener: Listen empathetically.

Pawsitivity Unleashed

72. Collaborate, Don't Compete: Work together.

73. Share Your Tricks: Share knowledge generously.

74. Create Harmony: Strive for balance.

75. Show Appreciation: Express gratitude.

76. Practice Generosity: Give freely.

77. Value Diversity: Embrace different perspectives.

78. Build Trust: Earn trust through honesty.

79. Stand Up for Others: Advocate for fairness.

80. Be Present in Relationships: Engage fully.

81. Bounce Back: Recover from setbacks.

82. Find the Silver Lining: See positives in challenges.

83. Learn from Challenges: Grow from difficulties.

84. Adopt a Growth Mindset: Believe in growth.

85. Stay Adaptable: Adjust to changes.

86. Lean on Your Pack: Seek support.

87. Stay Grounded in Storms: Find inner strength.

88. Maintain Hope: Believe in brighter days.

89. Do not Bark Up the Wrong Tree: Focus on solutions.

90. Channel Your Inner Doggedness: Be determined.

91. Weather Life's Seasons: Adapt to life's changes.

92. Build Emotional Resilience: Strengthen emotional strength.

93. View Challenges as Training: See challenges as growth opportunities.

94. Stay Centered in Chaos: Keep calm in turmoil.

95. Cultivate Inner Strength: Grow inner resilience.

96. Seek Guidance: Learn from mentors.

Pawsitivity Unleashed

97. Accept Impermanence: Embrace change.

98. Stay Persistent: Keep moving forward.

99. Practice Self-Compassion in Tough Times: Be kind to yourself.

100. Know When to Rest: Listen to your needs

After acquainting yourself with the principles of pawsitive living, let us now explore how they intertwine with your journey towards rediscovering, reinventing, and reclaiming your life with purpose and passion.

I have trodden this same path you are about to embark on, albeit it took me longer than thirty days as I did not have a guide or coach to provide me with the tools, share their experience or show me which resource would be ineffective. So, because of that I spent three decades collecting and researching and putting together the answers to all my questions on finding purpose and passion, and now you have all that knowledge in just a thirty-day journey. I took everything I learned, found, and uncovered, refined it, consolidated it, and discarded the elements that I tried, tested, and proved ineffective and now I want to give it to you. I wish I had had something like this years ago, however you do, and it will save you countless years because the answers are all here for you.

We all share the same journey of life, and on that journey are faced with challenges on specific topic whether it be relationships, money, career, personal development and more. I devised eleven categories that encompass these topics that we have humans face as we journey

Pawsitivity Unleashed

to our life we have always dreamed of. With my experience in coaching and training I coordinated the topics to match skillsets, and values and qualities that we would want to have or develop to help us achieve success in those areas. On your thirty-day journey you have a choice to choose anyone, two or all the life journey to pawsitive living to focus on reaching your ideal life you have always dreamed. Each journey encapsulates all the potential goals and aspirations one might have when seeking purpose and passion and each of these eleven categories encompasses the one hundred principles of pawsitive living.

The eleven journeys signify the fundamental areas of focus that contribute to a well-rounded and fulfilling life. Again, derived from the principles of pawsitive living, it has now been consolidated for you into this easy-to-follow guide. Below is the list of life journeys, along with the benefits they offer and the resolutions they can provide. Take a moment to review the journeys, and then the additional details following about each topic. After you choose the journey, the next section provides you with a goal checklist to follow to ensure you master that specific journey. Use that checklist as you work though the workbook/journal in your 30-day journey.

The Eleven Life Journeys to Pawsitive Living:

- *Mindset and Approach*

- *Communication and Connection*

- *Self-Development and Growth*

- *Relationships and Community*

- *Productivity and Success*

- *Resilience and Coping*

- *Health and Well-being*

- *Financial Management*

- *Personal Development*

- *Creativity and Innovation*

- *Leadership and Influence*

Pawsitivity Unleashed

A Journey of Mindset & Approach

The life journey of mindset and approach focuses on the attitudes and perspectives that shape how we approach life. This includes having a positive mindset, having a willingness to learn, remaining adaptable or having adaptability, and understanding and having gratitude which are all crucial for personal growth and overcoming challenges.

What is a Positive Mindset?

A *positive mindset* is foundational to how we interpret and react to the world around us. It involves cultivating an optimistic outlook, seeing challenges as opportunities, and maintaining hope even in difficult circumstances. A positive mindset can help someone learn to build resilience in the face of challenges, create and build optimism when they find they are pessimistic and can even offer additional health benefits, decreasing stress, decreasing fatigue and more.

What are the benefits to a positive mindset and approach?

- *Resilience:* The ability to build resilience, allowing you to bounce back from setbacks and failures with determination rather than being discouraged.
- *Optimism:* The ability to look at the brighter side of things helps you to maintain motivation and perseverance.

- *Health:* Studies have shown that a positive mindset can have tangible benefits on physical and mental health, reducing stress and promoting overall well-being.

Why is having a mindset open to learning and a willingness to learn essential for personal growth and development?

It builds:

- *Curiosity:* A desire to explore innovative ideas, perspectives, and experiences.
- *Adaptability:* The willingness to change one's views based on added information or experiences.
- *Humility:* The understanding that there is always more to learn and being open to feedback and constructive criticism.

Adaptability: Adaptability is the ability to adjust to new conditions and challenges.

It is about:

- *Flexibility:* Being able to change plans or approaches when necessary.
- *Problem-Solving:* Finding creative solutions to unexpected problems.
- *Resilience:* Adaptable, you can navigate uncertainty and change with greater ease.

Why is Gratitude important when working on mindset and approach?

Practicing gratitude involves acknowledging and appreciating the positive aspects of life, even amidst challenges.

It builds:

- *Perspective:* Gratitude helps shift focus from what is lacking to what is present and valuable.
- *Mental Health:* Regularly expressing gratitude has been linked to improved mental well-being, lower stress levels, and a more positive outlook on life.
- *Relationships:* Gratitude fosters stronger relationships, as it encourages acknowledgment of others' contributions and kindness.

Best Approachs to utilize with Mindset for Overcoming Challenges:

- *Problem-Solving:* Instead of getting overwhelmed by obstacles, a positive mindset focuses on finding solutions.
- *Learning from Failure:* With a willingness to learn, failures are seen as lessons rather than reasons to give up.
- *Adaptability in Change:* Life brings unexpected changes, and an adaptable mindset allows for smoother transitions.

- *Gratitude in Adversity:* Even in tough times, finding things to be grateful for can provide a sense of perspective and motivation to keep going.

How can you cultivate a positive mindset and positive approach?

- *Daily Practices:* Meditation, journaling, or affirmations can help reinforce positive thinking and gratitude.
- *Positive Surroundings:* Being around supportive and positive influences can shape our mindset.
- *Challenging Comfort Zones:* Trying new things and stepping out of comfort zones encourages adaptability and learning.
- *Seeking Growth:* Actively seeking out opportunities to gain experience, whether through books, courses, or experiences.
- *Mindfulness:* Being present in the moment helps appreciate the small joys and maintain perspective.

What does Cultivating a Positive Mindset and Approach Create?

- Resilience
- Optimism
- A growth-oriented perspective
- Personal growth
- Fulfillment

A Journey of Communication & Connection

Effective communication and connection with others are essential for building relationships, fostering understanding, and achieving mutual goals.

These principles emphasize:

- *Active Listening:* Active listening is more than just hearing words; it is about fully engaging with what others are saying. By giving someone your undivided attention, you show respect and a genuine interest in their perspective. This builds trust and encourages open dialogue.

Active listening involves:

- *Eye Contact:* Demonstrates attentiveness and interest.
- *Avoiding Interruptions:* Allows the speaker to convey their thoughts fully.
- *Reflecting and Clarifying*: Summarizing or asking questions to ensure understanding.
- *Empathy:* Empathy is the ability to understand and share the feelings of another person. It is the foundation of emotional intelligence and allows you to connect on a deeper level. When you empathize with someone:

- *Validation of Other Feelings:* Acknowledging emotions helps people feel heard and understood.
- *Building Trust:* Knowing that someone "gets" you creates a strong bond.
- *Creating Support:* Empathy often leads to actions that help ease someone's burden.

What is Clear Communication?

Clear communication is the cornerstone of any successful interaction. It ensures that your message is understood without confusion or misinterpretation.

Clear communication involves:

- *Being Concise:* Delivering your message in a straightforward manner.
- *Using Simple Language:* Avoiding jargon or complex terms that might confuse.
- *Checking for Understanding:* Asking questions like "Does that make sense?" ensures clarity.

What Does it Mean to Create a Supportive Environment?

A supportive environment is one where you feel safe, respected, and encouraged to express yourself.

Pawsitivity Unleashed

When you create a supportive environment:

- *People Thrive:* Create the feeling of being safe allows you to take risks, share ideas, and grow.
- *Conflict Resolution Improves:* Open communication means issues are addressed constructively.
- *Collaboration Soars:* Teams are more productive when everyone feels valued and supported.

What is the Importance Behind Building Relationships?

At its core, effective communication is about building and nurturing relationships. Whether with friends, family, colleagues, or clients:

- *Trust is Essential:* Trust forms the foundation of all relationships. Effective communication fosters trust.
- *Conflict Resolution:* Disagreements are inevitable, but how they are managed determines the strength of the relationship.
- *Mutual Goals:* Whether personal or professional, clear communication aligns everyone toward a common objective.

What is the Importance of Achieving Mutual Goals?

When communication is clear, and connections are strong:

- *Goals Are Aligned:* Everyone understands their role and how it contributes to the larger picture.

Pawsitivity Unleashed

- *Efficiency Increases:* Miscommunication leads to wasted time and effort; clear communication streamlines processes.
- *Innovation Flourishes:* A supportive environment encourages creative thinking and problem-solving.

These principles guide you to becoming a better communicator but also a better human. They foster understanding, respect, and collaboration, which are essential for navigating the complexities of relationships and achieving shared objectives.

A Journey of Self-Development & Growth

Self-development is key to reaching your greatest potential. These principles encourage continuous learning, goal setting, resilience, and self-care. They promote the idea that personal growth leads to a more fulfilling life.

Self-development is also the ongoing process of improving oneself mentally, emotionally, and physically. It involves cultivating skills, knowledge, and attitudes that contribute to personal growth and well-being.

These principles are crucial because they offer:

- *Continuous Learning:* Continuous learning is about seeking knowledge and skills throughout your life. It keeps the mind active, opens the doors to new possibilities, and helps you adapt to a changing world.

When you embrace continuous learning:

- *You Stay Relevant:* In a fast-paced world, learning new skills keeps you competitive in your field.
- *Personal Growth:* Learning challenges your mind and expands your perspective, leading to personal development.
- *Adaptability:* New knowledge helps you adapt to changes in your industry or environment.
- *Goal Setting:* Setting goals gives direction and purpose to your efforts. Whether short-term or long-term, goals provide motivation and focus.

When you set goals:

- *You Stay Motivated:* Goals give you something to work toward, keeping you energized and engaged.
- *Gain Clarity:* Clear goals help you make decisions aligned with your objectives.
- *Accountability:* Goals create a framework for tracking progress and adjusting as needed.

What is Resilience?

Resilience is the ability to bounce back from adversity stronger than before. It is about facing challenges with courage and maintaining a positive outlook.

When you cultivate resilience:

- *You Overcome Obstacles:* Resilience helps you navigate setbacks without losing momentum.
- *Emotional Well-being:* Resilient, you manage stress better and maintain a healthier perspective.
- *Growth Mindset:* Resilience is tied to a growth mindset, where failures are seen as learning opportunities.

What are the benefits of Self-Care?

Self-care involves taking deliberate actions to maintain and improve your physical, mental, and emotional health. It is not selfish; it is necessary for overall well-being.

When you practice self-care:

- *You Boost Productivity:* Taking breaks and managing stress improves focus and productivity.
- *Better Relationships:* When you are well-cared for, you can give more to others without burning out.

Pawsitivity Unleashed

- *Mind-Body Connection*: Self-care recognizes the interconnectedness of physical and mental health.

Does Following these Principles Really Lead to More Fulfillment in Life?

These principles collectively lead to a more fulfilling life because they offer:

- *Personal Growth:* Continuous learning and goal setting ensure you are always evolving and improving.
- *Build Resilience:* The ability to bounce back from setbacks means challenges do not derail your progress.
- *Create Self-Care:* Taking care of yourself ensures you have the energy and resilience to pursue your passions.
- <u>*Create Purpose*</u>: Setting and achieving goals gives life direction and meaning.

What are the Benefits of Self-Development?

- *Increased Confidence*: As you achieve goals and learn new skills, your confidence grows.
- *Improved Relationships:* When you are fulfilled and resilient, you bring a positive energy to your relationships.
- *Better Problem-Solving:* Continuous learning enhances your critical thinking skills, making you more effective.

- *Emotional Intelligence:* Self-development often includes improving emotional intelligence, which is vital for understanding and managing emotions.

Self-development is not just about acquiring knowledge or skills; it is about becoming the best version of yourself. It is a comprehensive approach that encompasses mental, emotional, and physical well-being. By embracing continuous learning, setting goals, building resilience, and practicing self-care, you pave the way for a more fulfilling and purposeful life.

A Journey of Relationships & Community

Healthy relationships and a dedicated support system are vital for emotional well-being and success. These principles highlight qualities like trust, loyalty, collaboration, and generosity, which contribute to positive interactions with others.

Trust

Trust is the foundation of any healthy relationship. When there is trust:

- *Openness Prevails:* People are more willing to be vulnerable and share their thoughts and feelings.
- *Conflict Resolution is Easier:* Trust allows for honest discussions about disagreements.

Pawsitivity Unleashed

- *Relationships Deepen:* Trust fosters intimacy and closeness.

Loyalty

Loyalty is the commitment to stand by someone's side through thick and thin. When loyalty is present:

- *Support is Assured:* Knowing someone is loyal means you can count on them in times of need.
- *Confidence Grows:* Loyalty builds confidence in relationships, knowing you have each other's backs.
- *Trust is Reinforced*: Loyalty and trust go hand in hand, reinforcing the bond between you.

Generosity

Generosity is about giving freely of your time, resources, and support. When you are generous:

- *Relationships Flourish:* Generosity fosters a sense of goodwill and reciprocity.
- *Trust is Built:* Generosity builds trust as it shows a willingness to invest in others.
- *Community is Created:* Acts of generosity create a positive environment where people support each other.

Emotional Well-Being

Healthy relationships and support systems are linked to emotional well-being:

- *Reduced Stress:* Knowing you have people you can rely on reduces stress levels.
- *Increased Happiness:* Positive interactions with others lead to greater happiness.
- *Better Mental Health:* Supportive relationships are a buffer against mental health issues.

Positive Interactions

Qualities like trust, loyalty, collaboration, and generosity create an environment where positive interactions thrive:

- *Mutual Respect:* These qualities foster mutual respect, essential for healthy relationships.
- *Conflict Resolution:* When conflicts arise, these qualities provide a framework for constructive resolution.
- *Celebrating Success:* In a supportive environment, achievements are celebrated together, fostering motivation and a sense of achievement.

These principles emphasize that healthy relationships and a dedicated support system are not just beneficial but essential for emotional well-being, personal growth, and success. They create a positive cycle where you can support each other, leading to a more fulfilling and meaningful life.

A Journey of Productivity & Success

To achieve goals and lead a productive life, certain principles such as time management, focus, adaptability, and celebrating achievements are crucial. This category emphasizes the habits and strategies that lead to success.

Why is Time Management important?

Effective time management is about making the most of the time available:

- *Prioritization:* Identifying and focusing on tasks that are most important and urgent.
- *Planning:* Creating schedules or to-do lists to allocate time efficiently.
- *Productivity Boost:* When time is managed well, productivity increases, leading to more tasks accomplished.
- *Reduced Stress:* Knowing how to manage time effectively reduces the stress of feeling overwhelmed.

What is the importance of Focus?

Maintaining focus is essential for completing tasks and achieving goals:

- *Eliminating Distractions*: Being able to concentrate without interruptions.
- *Quality Work:* Deep focus leads to higher-quality work and problem-solving.
- *Efficiency:* Tasks are completed more quickly and with fewer errors when focus is maintained.
- *Goal Alignment:* Focusing on tasks aligned with goals ensures progress in the right direction.

What is the importance of Adaptability?

Adaptability is the ability to adjust to changing circumstances and challenges:

- *Problem-Solving:* Being adaptable allows for creative solutions to unexpected problems.
- *Resilience:* When faced with setbacks, adaptability helps bounce back and find new paths.
- *Open-Mindedness:* Adaptable, you are open to innovative ideas and perspectives.
- *Continuous Improvement:* Being adaptable means being open to change and growth.

Pawsitivity Unleashed

Why is Celebrating Achievements an Important Aspect of Your Journey?

Acknowledging and celebrating successes is crucial for motivation and morale:

- *Motivation Boost:* Celebrating achievements reinforces positive behavior and motivates you for more.
- *Sense of Accomplishment:* Recognizing milestones provides a sense of progress and accomplishment.
- *Team Spirit:* Celebrating achievements as a team builds camaraderie and a sense of unity.
- *Positive Reinforcement:* Like a reward system, celebrating achievements reinforces desired behaviors.

What are the Benefits to Setting Goals?

Goal setting provides direction and purpose:

- *Clarity:* Clearly defined goals give a clear sense of direction.
- *Motivation:* Goals provide a target to strive towards, keeping motivation high.
- *Measurable Progress*: Having goals allows for tracking progress and adjusting.
- *Personal Growth:* Setting challenging goals encourages personal development and growth.

Why is it so Important to Reflect on Progress?

Regularly reflecting on progress allows for course correction and improvement:

- *Learning Opportunities:* Reflecting on both successes and failures provides valuable lessons.
- *Adjustments:* Reflection helps identify what is working and what needs to change.
- *Self-Awareness:* Through reflection, you gain a deeper understanding of their strengths and weaknesses.
- *Strategic Planning:* Reflection informs future actions and strategies.

How does Resilience Come into Play During This Process?

Resilience is the ability to bounce back from setbacks:

- *Persistence:* Resilience keeps you going despite obstacles.
- *Adaptability:* Resilient, you find ways to overcome challenges and adapt to new situations.
- *Emotional Strength:* Resilience helps manage stress and emotions during tough times.
- *Growth Mindset:* Resilience is rooted in a belief that setbacks are opportunities for growth.

Pawsitivity Unleashed

How is Productivity Affected or Important When Making Progress?

Productivity habits lead to efficient use of time and resources:

- *Efficient Workflows:* Productivity habits streamline processes for maximum output.
- *Eliminating Procrastination*: Productivity techniques help overcome procrastination.
- *Consistent Progress:* Productivity habits ensure steady progress towards goals.
- *Work-Life Balance*: Being productive allows for achieving more in less time, creating space for personal life.

How Does Adaptation to Change Affect Progress?

Adapting to change is crucial in a rapidly evolving world:

- *Flexibility:* Being able to adjust plans and strategies when circumstances change.
- *Innovation:* Adapting to change often leads to innovative solutions and ideas.
- *Resilience:* Adaptation to change builds resilience and the ability to thrive in uncertain times.
- *Competitive Advantage*: Organizations and you who can adapt quickly gain a competitive edge.

Why is it Important to Remain a Continuous Learner during your Progress Journey?

Continual learning keeps you ahead of the curve with:

- *Skill Development:* Learning new skills improves capabilities and employability.
- *Adaptability:* Learning new things fosters adaptability to modern technologies and trends.
- *Personal Growth*: Continuous learning leads to personal development and a broader perspective.
- *Innovation and Creativity:* Exposure to innovative ideas fuels innovation and creativity.

How does Celebration Benefit Progress?

Celebrating achievements is not just about the result but also about the journey:

- *Recognition:* Celebrating achievements recognizes the effort and dedication put in.
- *Team Building:* Celebrating as a team strengthens bonds and fosters a positive work culture.
- *Motivation:* Celebrations boost morale and motivation to keep striving for success.
- *Reflection:* Celebrating achievements allows for reflection on progress and growth.

Pawsitivity Unleashed

These principles emphasize the habits and strategies that contribute to your personal and professional success. They form the foundation for effective goal setting, productivity, resilience, and adaptability, all of which are essential for you to lead a productive and fulfilling life.

A Journey of Resilience & Coping

Life is full of challenges, and resilience helps navigate through them. These principles focus on bouncing back from setbacks, finding positives in tricky situations, seeking support, and maintaining hope during tough times.

How do you Learn to Bounce Back from Setbacks?

- *Positive Mindset:* Resilience starts with a positive outlook, seeing setbacks as temporary and manageable.
- *Learning from Failure:* Resilient you view failures as learning opportunities, extracting valuable lessons for future endeavors.
- *Adaptability:* Resilience is about being flexible and adaptive to change, adjusting plans and strategies as needed.
- *Critical Thinking Skills:* Resilience fosters the ability to tackle challenges head-on, finding creative solutions to obstacles.

Why is it Best to Find Positives not Negatives in Difficult Situations?

- *Silver Linings:* Resilient people look for positive aspects in tough situations, finding something positive even amidst adversity.
- *Gratitude Practice:* Cultivating gratitude helps shift focus from challenges to blessings, fostering resilience.
- *Perspective Shift:* Resilience involves shifting perspectives to see difficulties as opportunities for growth and self-discovery.
- *Optimism:* A resilient mindset leans towards optimism, believing that things will improve despite current challenges.

What are the Benefits to Seeking Support?

- *Building a Support Network:* Resilient you surround themselves with supportive friends, family, or colleagues.
- *Openness to Help:* Being resilient means recognizing when to ask for help, whether it is emotional support or practical assistance.
- *Professional Guidance:* Seeking advice from mentors or professionals is a sign of resilience, acknowledging that expertise can provide valuable insights.
- *Mutual Support:* Resilience in communities comes from mutual support, where you lean on each other during tough times.

How do you Maintain Hope During Tough Times?

- **Belief in Better Days:** Resilience is grounded in the belief that challenging times are temporary and that brighter days lie ahead.
- *Staying Grounded:* Resilient, you maintain a sense of grounding, finding stability amidst turmoil.
- *Mindfulness Practice:* Being present in the moment helps manage stress and anxiety during tough times.
- *Self-Encouragement:* Resilience involves self-encouragement, reminding oneself of past successes and strengths.

What are Some Coping Strategies to utilize on a transformational Journey?

- *Emotional Regulation:* Resilient people have healthy coping mechanisms to manage stress and emotions effectively.
- *Self-Care:* Prioritizing self-care, such as exercise, adequate sleep, and relaxation techniques, is crucial for resilience.
- *Acceptance of Imperfection:* Resilience involves accepting imperfections and understanding that setbacks are a natural part of life.
- *Patience:* Resilient, you have patience with themselves and the process of overcoming challenges.

What is Resilience Building Activities?

- **Journaling**: Writing down thoughts and feelings can be therapeutic and help process emotions.

Pawsitivity Unleashed

- *Physical Exercise:* Regular exercise not only boosts physical health but also improves mood and resilience.
- *Meditation and Mindfulness:* These practices cultivate inner strength and calmness, essential for resilience.
- *Engaging in Hobbies:* Activities that bring joy and passion can serve as outlets during tough times.

Why is Accepting Change important to a transformational Journey?

- *Flexibility:* Resilient, you are flexible and able to adapt to changing circumstances.
- *Embracing Uncertainty:* Resilience involves being comfortable with the unknown and embracing life's unpredictability.
- *Letting Go of Control:* Understanding that some things are beyond control allows for resilience in the face of uncertainty.
- *Finding Opportunities in Change:* Resilient people see change as an opportunity for growth and new experiences.

How do you learn to Embrace Setbacks as Learning Opportunities?

- *Failure as Feedback:* Resilience involves seeing failures as feedback, not as a reflection of self-worth.
- *Iterative Improvement:* Resilient you continually refine their approaches based on past experiences.
- *Redefining Success:* Resilience challenges conventional definitions of success, focusing on personal growth and development.

- *Celebrating Progress:* Even small steps forward are celebrated as signs of resilience and determination.

These principles of resilience focus on the attitudes, behaviors, and coping strategies that help you bounce back from setbacks and help you find strength in adversity, seek support when needed, and maintain hope during challenging times. They help to form the foundation for building inner strength and navigating life's difficulties with resilience and grace.

A Journey of Health & Well-being

Physical and mental health are the foundation of a fulfilling life. Hydration, rest, exercise, mental stimulation, and gratitude contribute to overall well-being, enabling you to thrive in all areas of life.

What does Physical Health look like?

- *Hydration:* Drinking an adequate amount of water is essential for bodily functions, including digestion, circulation, and temperature regulation.

o *Benefits:* Proper hydration improves energy levels, cognitive function, and overall health.

- *Rest and Sleep:* Sufficient rest and quality sleep are crucial for physical recovery, immune function, and mental well-being.

o *Benefits:* Restorative sleep supports mood regulation, memory consolidation, and overall cellular repair.

- *Exercise:* Regular physical activity improves cardiovascular health, muscle strength, and flexibility.

o *Benefits:* Exercise releases endorphins, reducing stress, anxiety, and symptoms of depression.

- *Nutrition*: Consuming a balanced diet rich in nutrients fuels the body for optimal function.

o *Benefits:* Proper nutrition supports immune health, brain function, and overall vitality.

- *Sunshine Exposure:* Moderate exposure to sunlight promotes the production of Vitamin D, essential for bone health and mood regulation.

o *Benefits:* Sunlight boosts serotonin levels, improving mood and combating seasonal affective disorder.

What does Mental Health look like?

- *Mental Stimulation:* Engaging in intellectually stimulating activities, such as reading, puzzles, or learning new skills, keeps the mind sharp.

o *Benefits:* Mental stimulation supports cognitive function, memory retention, and creativity.

- *Gratitude Practice:* Cultivating a sense of gratitude through journaling or reflection fosters positive emotions and resilience.

o *Benefits:* Gratitude reduces stress, improves sleep quality, and enhances overall well-being.

- *Mindfulness and Meditation:* These practices promote mental clarity, emotional regulation, and stress reduction.

o *Benefits:* Mindfulness reduces anxiety, improves focus, and enhances self-awareness.

- *Social Connections:* Maintaining meaningful relationships and social interactions supports mental health.

o *Benefits:* Social connections reduce feelings of loneliness, depression, and anxiety.

- *Therapy and Counseling:* Seeking professional help when needed promotes emotional healing and growth.

o *Benefits:* Therapy provides tools for managing stress, processing emotions, and improving self-esteem.

What does Holistic Well-Being look like?

- *Balance:* Balancing work, rest, play, and personal time creates harmony in life.

o *Benefits:* Balance prevents burnout, improves productivity, and fosters overall life satisfaction.

- *Self-Care:* Prioritizing self-care activities, such as hobbies, relaxation, or pampering, nurtures the soul.

o *Benefits:* Self-care boosts self-esteem, reduces stress, and promotes emotional resilience.

- *Physical Check-Ups:* Regular medical check-ups and screenings are crucial for early detection of health issues.

o *Benefits:* Early detection allows for timely treatment, improving health outcomes and longevity.

Pawsitivity Unleashed

- *Healthy Habits:* Developing healthy routines, such as a morning routine or exercise regimen, creates stability and discipline.

o *Benefits:* Healthy habits lead to increased energy, improved mood, and better overall health.

- *Gratitude for the Body:* Appreciating one's body and its capabilities promotes body positivity and self-acceptance.

o *Benefits:* Body appreciation fosters a healthy relationship with food, exercise, and self-image.

What Can You Do to Increase Resilience Against Stress?

- *Stress Management:* Learning stress-reduction techniques, such as deep breathing or yoga, improves resilience.

o *Benefits:* Stress management techniques reduce cortisol levels, enhance relaxation, and improve overall health.

- *Boundaries:* Setting healthy boundaries in personal and professional life protects mental and emotional well-being.

o *Benefits:* Boundaries prevent burnout, reduce conflict, and improve relationships.

Pawsitivity Unleashed

- *Art and Creativity:* Engaging in creative pursuits, such as painting, music, or writing, provides an outlet for emotions and self-expression.

o *Benefits:* Creativity reduces stress, improves mood, and enhances critical thinking skills.

- *Nature Connection:* Spending time in nature, known as ecotherapy, reduces stress and promotes well-being.

o *Benefits*: Nature exposure lowers blood pressure, improves mood, and boosts immune function.

What is Some Preventative Health Measures to Take on a Health and Wellness Journey?

- *Vaccinations and Immunizations:* Staying up to date with vaccinations protects against preventable diseases.

o *Benefits:* Vaccinations prevent illness, reduce healthcare costs, and protect vulnerable populations.

- *Screenings and Tests:* Regular health screenings, such as blood pressure checks or cholesterol tests, detect health issues early.

118

o *Benefits:* Early detection allows for prompt treatment, improving health outcomes and quality of life.

• *Healthy Aging:* Adopting healthy lifestyle habits throughout life promotes successful aging and longevity.

o *Benefits:* Healthy aging reduces the risk of chronic diseases, maintains independence, and improves quality of life.

• *Mental Health Days:* Taking mental health days when needed allows for rest and rejuvenation.

o *Benefits*: Mental health days reduce burnout, improve focus, and enhance overall well-being.

What are Ways you can Cultivate Joy and Fulfillment on a Health and Wellness Journey?

• *Pursuing Passions:* Engaging in activities that bring joy and fulfillment nurtures mental health.

o *Benefits:* Pursuing passions boosts happiness, reduces stress, and provides a sense of purpose.

• *Acts of Kindness:* Performing random acts of kindness for others creates a sense of fulfillment and connection.

Pawsitivity Unleashed

o *Benefits:* Kindness releases feel-good hormones, such as oxytocin, improving mood and well-being.

- ***Laughter and Humor:*** Incorporating laughter and humor into daily life lightens the mood and reduces stress.

o *Benefits:* Laughter releases endorphins, improves immune function, and enhances social bonds.

By focusing on physical and mental health, you can create a solid foundation for a fulfilling life. These principles promote vitality, resilience, emotional well-being, and a sense of balance that allows you to thrive in all aspects of your life.

A Journey of Financial Management

Sound financial principles are essential for stability and security. Budgeting, saving, investing, and seeking advice ensure financial health and reduce stress related to money matters.

<u>Budgeting</u>

- ***Financial Awareness:*** Budgeting is the foundation of financial health, providing a clear understanding of income and expenses.

- *Expense Tracking:* It involves tracking spending habits to identify areas for saving and potential cutbacks.
- *Goal Setting*: Budgeting helps set specific financial goals, whether it is saving for a vacation, buying a home, or retirement.
- *Emergency Funds:* Budgeting includes allocating funds for unexpected expenses, creating a safety net for emergencies.

Saving

- *Building Reserves:* Saving regularly builds financial reserves for future needs, such as emergencies, major purchases, or retirement.
- *Automatic Savings:* Setting up automatic transfers to savings accounts ensures consistency and discipline in saving habits.
- *Short-Term vs. Long-Term:* Saving accounts for both short-term goals (like a vacation) and long-term goals (like retirement).

Investing

- *Wealth Growth:* Investing allows money to grow over time through various vehicles such as stocks, bonds, mutual funds, or real estate.
- *Diversification:* Investing in different assets reduces risk and increases potential returns.
- *Understanding Risk Tolerance:* You should invest according to their risk tolerance and financial goals.

- *Compound Interest:* Investing early harnesses the power of compound interest, leading to substantial wealth accumulation over time.

Seeking Advice

- *Financial Literacy:* Seeking advice means continuously educating oneself about financial matters, including savings, investments, and debt management.
- *Professional Guidance:* Consulting financial advisors or planners helps create personalized financial plans based on individual circumstances.
- *Risk Assessment:* Professionals can assess risk tolerance and recommend suitable investment strategies.
- *Tax Planning:* Advisors provide guidance on tax-efficient strategies, maximizing returns while minimizing tax liabilities.

Debt Management

- *Reducing Debt:* Sound financial principles include strategies for reducing and managing debt, such as credit card balances, loans, and mortgages.
- *Interest Rates:* Understanding interest rates and their impact on debt repayment is crucial for financial health.
- *Debt Repayment Plans:* Creating structured plans to pay off debts systematically, starting with high-interest debts.

- *Avoiding Unnecessary Debt:* Making informed decisions to avoid accumulating unnecessary debt, such as impulse purchases or high interest loans

Long-Term Financial Planning

- *Retirement Planning:* Sound financial principles emphasize early and consistent retirement planning through retirement accounts like 401(k)s or IRAs.
- *Estate Planning:* It involves creating wills, trusts, and other legal documents to ensure assets are distributed according to wishes.
- *Healthcare Planning:* Considering healthcare costs in retirement and planning for medical expenses is crucial for financial stability.
- *Life Insurance:* Having adequate life insurance coverage protects loved ones in case of unexpected events.

Financial Security

- *Peace of Mind:* Following these principles leads to financial security, reducing stress and anxiety related to money matters.
- *Financial Independence:* Sound financial practices pave the way for financial independence, where you have control over their financial future.
- *Flexibility and Freedom:* Financial health allows for more flexibility and freedom in life choices, such as career changes or pursuing passions.

- *Generational Wealth:* Building wealth through sound financial principles enables the creation of generational wealth, benefiting future generations.

The Importance of Continuous Learning in Finance

- *Staying Informed:* Financial literacy is an ongoing process, staying updated on economic trends, investment strategies, and financial news.
- *Educational Resources:* Utilizing books, online resources, workshops, and seminars to expand financial knowledge.
- *Peer Learning:* Engaging in discussions with peers about financial experiences and strategies for growth.

Philanthropy and giving

- *Charitable Contributions:* Sound financial principles include giving back to society through charitable donations, supporting causes that align with personal values.
- *Impact Investing:* Investing in socially responsible funds or companies that promote positive social and environmental impacts.
- *Legacy Planning:* Incorporating charitable giving into estate planning, leaving a legacy of philanthropy.

These sound financial principles encompass budgeting, saving, investing, seeking advice, debt management, and long-term planning. They provide a roadmap for achieving financial stability,

Pawsitivity Unleashed

security, and the freedom to pursue one's life goals and dreams without undue financial stress.

A Journey of Personal Development

Personal growth goes beyond just learning. Travel, volunteering, hobbies, and cultural exploration enrich experiences and perspectives, leading to a more fulfilling life.

What is the Importance of Travel in a Personal Development Journey?

- *Broadening Perspectives:* Travel exposes you to diverse cultures, languages, and ways of life, fostering open-mindedness and understanding.
- *Cultural Immersion:* Engaging with locals and experiencing their customs firsthand provides deep insights into different lifestyles.
- *Stepping Out of Comfort Zones:* Travel challenges you to adapt to new environments, enhancing resilience and critical thinking skills.
- *Self-Discovery:* Traveling solo or with others encourages self-reflection and self-discovery, leading to personal growth.
- *Appreciation for Diversity:* Experiencing different cuisines, traditions, and landscapes cultivates an appreciation for the world's diversity.

- *Memorable Experiences:* Creating lasting memories and stories from travel adventures enriches life's narrative and creates a sense of fulfillment.

What is the Importance of Volunteering in a Personal Development Journey?

- *Giving Back:* Volunteering allows you to contribute to causes they are enthusiastic about, making a positive impact on communities.
- *Empathy and Compassion:* Working directly with those in need fosters empathy and compassion, enhancing emotional intelligence.
- *Skill Development:* Volunteering offers opportunities to develop new skills or apply existing skills in meaningful ways, boosting confidence.
- *Building Connections:* Volunteering often involves teamwork and collaboration, creating lasting friendships and professional networks.
- *Perspective Shifts:* Seeing the world from others' perspectives, especially those facing challenges, brings gratitude and humility.
- *Sense of Purpose:* Volunteering provides a sense of purpose and fulfillment, knowing one is making a difference in the lives of others.

What is the importance of Hobbies in a Personal Development Journey?

- *Stress Relief:* Engaging in hobbies provides a healthy outlet for stress and promotes mental well-being.
- *Creativity and Innovation:* Hobbies such as painting, writing, or crafting foster creativity and innovative thinking.
- *Continuous Learning*: Hobbies offer opportunities to gain experience new skills or deepen existing ones, promoting personal development.
- *Work-Life Balance:* Spending time on hobbies enhances work-life balance, preventing burnout and increasing overall happiness.
- *Social Connections:* Joining hobby groups or clubs introduces you to like-minded people, building social connections.
- *Achievement and Satisfaction:* Progressing in a hobby, whether mastering a musical instrument or completing a DIY project, brings a sense of achievement and satisfaction.

What is the Importance of Cultural Exploration in a Personal Development Journey?

- *Understanding Diversity:* Exploring diverse cultures promotes tolerance and understanding of diverse customs and traditions.
- *Cultural Appreciation:* Learning about art, music, literature, and history from various cultures enriches one's appreciation for the world's heritage.

- *Language Learning:* Immersing oneself in a new language through cultural exploration opens doors to communication and deeper connections.
- *Culinary Adventures:* Trying diverse cuisines introduces new flavors and expands culinary horizons, creating memorable experiences.
- *Historical Insights:* Visiting historical sites and museums provides insights into world history and how it has shaped societies.
- *Celebrating Similarities and Differences:* Cultural exploration highlights both the commonalities and unique aspects of human societies, fostering respect and unity.

What is the Importance of Personal Growth and Fulfillment in a Personal Development Journey?

- *Self-Expression:* Engaging in travel, volunteering, hobbies, and cultural exploration allows you to express themselves authentically.
- *Life Balance:* These activities contribute to a well-rounded life, balancing work, personal interests, and social connections.
- *Overcoming Challenges:* Each of these pursuits presents challenges that you must overcome, promoting resilience and growth.
- *Living in the Moment:* Whether exploring a new city, teaching a skill to others through volunteering, or indulging in a hobby, these activities encourage living in the present.

- *Life Enrichment:* Collecting experiences from travel, volunteering, hobbies, and cultural exploration creates a rich tapestry of memories and personal growth.
- *Gratitude and Happiness:* Engaging in these activities often leads to a greater sense of gratitude for life's experiences, contributing to overall happiness and fulfillment.

Travel, volunteering, hobbies, and cultural exploration are avenues for personal growth and enrichment. They provide opportunities to gain experience, connect with others, gain new perspectives, and create lasting memories. By engaging in these activities, you can lead a more fulfilling life, filled with meaningful experiences and a deeper understanding of yourself and the world around you.

A Journey of Creativity & Innovation

Creativity is the spark of innovation and problem-solving. These principles encourage brainstorming, collaboration, feedback, and open-mindedness to generate innovative ideas and solutions.

Benefits to Brainstorming

- *Free Idea Generation:* Brainstorming involves generating ideas freely without judgment.
- *Diverse Perspectives:* Encouraging diverse perspectives during brainstorming sessions leads to a wider range of ideas.

- *Quantity Over Quality:* Initially, focusing on generating a large quantity of ideas helps explore various possibilities.
- *Building on Ideas:* Participants can build on each other's ideas, creating innovative solutions through collaboration.

Benefits to Collaboration

- *Teamwork:* Collaboration brings together diverse skills and expertise to work towards a common goal.
- *Combining Strengths:* Each team member contributes unique strengths and perspectives, enhancing the quality of ideas.
- *Constructive collaboration:* Collaborative efforts often result in synergistic outcomes where the whole is greater than the sum of its parts.
- *Shared Ownership:* When ideas are co-created, team members feel a sense of ownership and are more motivated to execute them.

Benefits to Feedback

- *Constructive Criticism:* Feedback provides valuable insights for improvement without discouraging creativity.
- *Refinement:* Receiving feedback allows ideas to be refined and polished for better outcomes.
- *Iterative Process:* Continuous feedback loops help in iterating ideas, improving them with each cycle.
- *Validation:* Positive feedback validates innovative ideas, boosting confidence and enthusiasm.

Pawsitivity Unleashed

Benefits to Open-Mindedness

- *Acceptance of New Ideas:* Being open-minded means considering ideas that may initially seem unconventional.
- *Exploration of Alternatives:* Open-mindedness leads to exploring alternative perspectives and solutions.
- *Challenging Assumptions:* It involves questioning assumptions and norms to break away from traditional thinking.
- *Flexibility: Open-minded,* you are flexible in their thinking, adapting to added information and insights.

Benefits to having the abilities to Problem-Solve

- *Creative Solutions:* Creativity in problem-solving means thinking freely to find novel solutions.
- *Root Cause Analysis:* Identifying root causes of problems allows for targeted and innovative solutions.
- *Design Thinking:* Applying design thinking principles involves empathizing with users, defining problems, ideating solutions, prototyping, and testing.
- *Out-of-the-Box Thinking:* Creativity encourages exploring unconventional approaches that may lead to breakthrough solutions.

Benefits to Iterative Improvement

Iterative improvement involves repeatedly performing an action with the aim of enhancing it. This approach enables us to adjust the features of a product throughout the process, preventing the creation of something that includes only the features initially deemed necessary but is not suitable for its intended purpose. The benefits to using iterative process in your own journey includes:

- *Continuous Refinement of skill and self:* Ideas are refined through a series of iterations, improving them based on feedback and testing.

- *Agile Methodology:* Applying agile principles allows for quick iterations and adaptations to changing needs in a team environment. The agile methodology has been successfully used with large teams to take one project and break it down over 4 weeks, create adaptations and still align with customer goals. Applying the same methodology to your journey would support your goals.

- *Fail Fast, Learn Faster:* Encouraging experimentation and learning from failures leads to faster innovation.

- *Kaizen Philosophy:* The concept of continuous improvement ensures that even small enhancements lead to considerable progress over time individually or in a team environment. You begin with a project and build onto it rather than break it down with agile methodology. It has been successfully used in Japanese cultures and business all over the world and using this style journey has its own benefits as well.

For a clearer understanding, Agile Methodology is an approach to project management that emphasizes flexibility, collaboration, and rapid iteration. It is based on a set of principles that prioritize customer satisfaction, adaptive planning, and the delivery of working products in short time frames.

By applying agile principles, teams can break down projects into smaller increments, called iterations or sprints, typically lasting 1-4 weeks. During these iterations, teams plan, execute, and deliver small portions of the project, allowing for continuous feedback and improvement. This iterative process enables quick adaptations to changing needs or priorities, meaning you start with one big project, and you break it down into smaller projects still holding on to the goal of the customer.

Overall, Agile Methodology provides a framework for teams to deliver high-quality products efficiently while remaining responsive to customer needs and market changes.

The Kaizen Philosophy, rooted in the Japanese approach to business, emphasizes the continuous pursuit of improvement. This means that even the smallest enhancements can lead to significant progress over time. Originating as a methodology in the 1980s, Kaizen encourages change from any employee at any point in time, supporting the idea of "change for the better" or continuous improvement. Developed over decades, it was formally introduced to the world through the best-selling book "KAIZEN™" by Masaaki Imai, the founder of Kaizen Institute. Major companies like Toyota, Sony, Canon, Honda, Samsung, JTI, and Panasonic have implemented Kaizen to enhance their manufacturing processes.

In today's fiercely competitive global business environment, organizations are constantly seeking ways to refine their operations and maintain a leading edge. This style starts with a product and builds onto it. Both styles have the same outcomes, just a different process. Like life, we have different choices on how to choose the path to reclaim and reinvent ourselves. So, whether you pull the pieces apart and put them back together or start from the bottom and work your way up, your goal will still be the same.

What are the Benefits to Creativity in Daily Life?

•*Creative Problem-Solving:* Applying creative thinking to everyday challenges leads to more efficient and innovative solutions.

•*Artistic Expression:* Engaging in artistic hobbies like painting, writing, or music nurtures creativity and provides a creative outlet.

•*Innovative Approaches:* From cooking to home organization, creativity can enhance various aspects of daily life.

•*Mindfulness Practices:* Mindfulness and meditation foster creativity by clearing the mind and allowing innovative ideas to emerge.

What is important to have Playfulness and Exploration on your journey?

•*Curiosity:* Curiosity drives exploration and discovery, leading to innovative ideas and perspectives.

•*Playful Approach:* Approaching tasks with a playful mindset encourages experimentation and creativity.

•*Childlike Wonder:* Embracing a childlike wonder about the world fosters creativity and imagination.

•*Embracing Mistakes:* Seeing mistakes as opportunities for learning and growth encourages risk-taking and innovation.

What is the Importance of Creativity in Business?

•*Innovative Products/Services:* Creative thinking leads to the development of unique and marketable products or services.

•*Marketing and Branding:* Creativity in marketing strategies and branding sets businesses apart from competitors.

•*Problem Identification:* Creativity helps in identifying market gaps and customer needs that can be addressed through new offerings.

•*Employee Engagement*: Encouraging creativity among employees leads to a more engaged and motivated workforce.

What is the Importance of Creativity and Well-Being?

•*Stress Relief:* Engaging in creative activities can serve as a form of stress relief and relaxation.

•*Enhanced Mental Health:* Creativity has been linked to improved mental health and emotional well-being.

•*Personal Growth:* Exploring one's creative side fosters personal growth, self-discovery, and a sense of fulfillment.

•*Community and Connection:* Creative pursuits often lead to forming connections with like-minded you and communities.

Creativity is a multifaceted trait that can be nurtured and applied in various aspects of life. Whether in problem-solving, innovation, personal expression, or business strategy, fostering creativity through brainstorming, collaboration, feedback, and open-mindedness can lead to novel ideas, innovative solutions, and a more fulfilling life.

A Journey of Leadership & Influence

Effective leadership is about inspiring others and navigating challenges. These principles cover leading by example, clear communication, empowerment, problem-solving, vision, inspiration, decision-making, and conflict resolution.

What does Leading by Example Create?

•*Integrity:* Leaders set the tone for the team by demonstrating honesty, integrity, and ethical behavior in all actions.

•*Consistency:* Consistency in words and actions builds trust and credibility among team members.

•*Work Ethic:* Leading by example involves showing dedication, resilience, and a strong work ethic in pursuing goals.

•*Accountability:* Leaders hold themselves accountable for their actions and decisions, setting a standard for accountability within the team.

What does Clear Communication Create?

•*Transparency:* Transparent communication fosters trust and ensures everyone is on the same page regarding goals, expectations, and challenges.

•*Active Listening:* Effective leaders actively listen to the concerns, ideas, and feedback of team members, demonstrating empathy and understanding.

•*Clarity:* Clear and concise communication helps avoid misunderstandings and confusion, enabling efficient workflow and decision-making.

•*Feedback Loop:* Establishing an open feedback loop encourages continuous improvement and fosters a culture of learning and growth.

What does Empowerment Create?

•*Delegation:* Empowering team members involves delegating tasks and responsibilities based on individual strengths and skills, fostering autonomy and ownership.

•*Support:* Providing the necessary resources, guidance, and support empowers you to take initiative and achieve their full potential.

•*Recognition:* Recognizing and celebrating the contributions and achievements of team members reinforces their value and motivates continued excellence.

•*Development:* Investing in the development and growth of team members through training, mentoring, and opportunities for advancement empowers them to reach new heights.

What Does Problem-Solving Create?

•*Adaptability:* Effective leaders navigate challenges and change with flexibility and adaptability, finding creative solutions to complex problems.

•*Analytical Thinking:* Applying analytical thinking and critical thinking skills enables leaders to assess situations objectively and make informed decisions.

•*Collaboration:* Collaboration encourages diverse perspectives and expertise, leading to innovative problem-solving and better outcomes.

•*Resilience:* Leaders demonstrate resilience in the face of setbacks, inspiring confidence, and determination in their team members.

Pawsitivity Unleashed

What Does Vision Create?

•*Inspiring Vision:* A compelling vision inspires and motivates others, providing a sense of purpose and direction.

•*Strategic Planning:* Leaders develop strategic plans aligned with the vision, setting clear goals and milestones to chart the course forward.

•*Alignment:* Ensuring alignment between individual goals and the overarching vision fosters unity of purpose and collective effort.

•*Communication of Vision:* Articulating the vision clearly and consistently reinforces its importance and rallies support from stakeholders.

What Does Inspiration Create?

•*Leading with Passion*: Passion and enthusiasm are contagious, inspiring others to give their best and pursue excellence.

•*Storytelling:* Effective leaders use storytelling to convey the vision, values, and mission in a way that resonates emotionally and inspires action.

•*Role Modeling:* Modeling desirable behaviors and attitudes inspires others to emulate those qualities, creating a positive ripple effect within the organization.

•*Celebrating Successes:* Celebrating milestones and successes reinforces the shared vision and energizes the team to tackle new challenges.

What Does Decision-Making Create?

•*Strategic Decision-Making:* Leaders make well-informed decisions that align with the organization's goals and values, considering both short-term and long-term implications.

•*Decisiveness:* Decisive leaders have the courage to make tough decisions in a timely manner, even in the face of uncertainty or adversity.

•*Risk Management:* Effective decision-making involves assessing risks and weighing potential outcomes to mitigate risks while maximizing opportunities.

•*Transparency in Decision-Making:* Transparent decision-making processes foster trust and accountability, promoting acceptance and commitment from stakeholders.

What Does Conflict Resolution Create?

•*Active Mediation:* Effective leaders address conflicts promptly and impartially, facilitating constructive dialogue and finding mutually acceptable solutions.

•*Emotional Intelligence*: Leaders with high emotional intelligence empathize with conflicting parties, understanding underlying emotions and perspectives to resolve disputes effectively.

•*Fairness*: Leaders ensure fairness and equity in conflict resolution, upholding principles of justice and respect for all you involved.

•*Turning Conflict into Opportunity*: Transforming conflicts into opportunities for learning and growth strengthens relationships and fosters a culture of collaboration and resilience.

Pawsitivity Unleashed

Effective leadership is about inspiring and empowering others, fostering clear communication and collaboration, navigating challenges with resilience and strategic thinking, and creating a shared vision that motivates action and drives success. Leaders who lead by example, communicate effectively, empower their teams, solve problems creatively, articulate a compelling vision, inspire others, make sound decisions, and resolve conflicts constructively are well-positioned to achieve their goals and bring out the best in those they lead.

Now that we have delved into the one hundred principles of Pawsitive Living and explored the eleven possible journeys that can infuse purpose and passion back into our lives, you might have identified a few journeys that resonate deeply with you and hold significant meaning. These are the ones you may want to focus on over the next 30 days. In this section, I will outline the specific goals for each journey. Use this as a reference as you continue your work in your workbook and journal. As you achieve these goals, check them off your list and reflect on your progress. Use it as a tool to track your thoughts and emotions throughout the process. When you complete a journey, take a moment to reflect: Do you feel any different than when you started?

Reflecting on my own journey, I realize how beneficial having this structured approach would have been. It is something I use now and find incredibly helpful as a check-in tool. After six months or a year, revisiting these goals can offer valuable insights. If you can still check off all the points, it is a sign of maintaining progress. However, if you find yourself unable to, it is an indicator that certain thoughts, feelings, or emotions may have crept in, affecting your productivity or success on the journey. In such cases, it might be time for a reboot or a refresh of the skills, which I personally do quite often. We all need these check-ins as life happens, and the world around us can get busy, causing us to slip on tasks and structures.

The key is recognizing these shifts, acknowledging the changes, and taking proactive steps to get back on track. Remember, you are doing all this work for yourself – to feel good, to achieve better health mentally, physically, emotionally, and spiritually. It is all part of a process, not about achieving perfection but embracing the journey itself.

Goals for a Positive Mindset and Approach

- ☐ Start with a Wag: Approach each day with a cheerful outlook.
- ☐ See the Tail Wag: Look for good in every situation.
- ☐ Embrace the Learning Curve: Every experience is an opportunity to gain experience.
- ☐ Paws for Reflection: Take time to reflect on experiences.
- ☐ Tailor Your Approach: Adapt your approach to situations.
- ☐ Stay Pawsitive: Maintain a positive outlook.
- ☐ Treat Life as a Training Session: See challenges as opportunities.
- ☐ Celebrate Small Victories: Acknowledge every success.
- ☐ Trust the Process: Believe in the process of growth.
- ☐ Embrace Imperfection: Focus on progress, not perfection.
- ☐ Practice Gratitude: Be thankful for the positives.
- ☐ Focus on Solutions, Not Problems: Troubleshoot challenges.
- ☐ Welcome New Tricks: Be open to learning.
- ☐ Tailor Your Treats: Reward yourself appropriately.
- ☐ Consistent Kindness: Approach interactions with kindness.
- ☐ Live in the Moment: Embrace the present.
- ☐ Training Takes Time: Be patient with progress.
- ☐ Redirect, Don't Punish: Focus on positive actions.
- ☐ Reward Effort: Acknowledge challenging work.
- ☐ Cultivate Curiosity: Stay open-minded.

Goals for Communication and Connection

- ☐ Listen with Your "Dog Ears": Truly listen to others.
- ☐ Use Your Non-Verbal "Tail Wag": Positive body language is key.
- ☐ Communicate Clearly: Be direct and honest.
- ☐ Use Positive Reinforcement: Encourage good behavior.
- ☐ Be an Active Listener: Engage fully in conversations.
- ☐ Speak Kindly: Use gentle words.
- ☐ Teach by Example: Lead with your actions.
- ☐ Tailor Your "Commands": Adjust communication styles.
- ☐ Create a Safe Space: Foster a safe environment.
- ☐ Show Affection: Offer genuine love and appreciation.
- ☐ Use Positive Words: Speak positively.
- ☐ Empathize with Others: Understand their perspective.
- ☐ Teach, Don't Preach: Share knowledge inspiringly.
- ☐ Stay Present in Conversations: Give full attention.
- ☐ Find Common Ground: Build connections.
- ☐ Acknowledge Others' Strengths: Appreciate talents.
- ☐ Offer Encouragement: Support others.
- ☐ Stay Calm in Conflict: Handle conflicts calmly.
- ☐ Apologize When Necessary: Be humble and apologize.

Goals for Self-Development and Growth

☐ Foster Trust: Build trust through honesty.

☐ Stay Playful: Keep a playful spirit.

☐ Seek Feedback: Learn from feedback.

☐ Challenge Yourself: Push beyond comfort zones.

☐ Adapt and Evolve: Adjust to change.

☐ Invest in Learning: Never stop growing.

☐ Set "Training" Goals: Define clear objectives.

☐ Embrace Diversity: Celebrate differences.

☐ Practice Self-Compassion: Be kind to yourself.

☐ Stay Persistent: Keep going despite challenges.

☐ Visualize Success: Imagine achieving goals.

☐ Take Breaks: Rest and recharge.

☐ Stay Healthy: Prioritize well-being.

☐ Learn from Failure: See failure as a lesson.

☐ Practice Mindfulness: Stay present.

☐ Stay Flexible: Adapt to changes.

☐ Cultivate Resilience: Bounce back from setbacks.

☐ Visualize Positivity: Focus on positive outcomes.

☐ Celebrate Self-Improvement: Acknowledge growth.

☐ Stay Grounded: Remain humble.

☐ Stay Inspired: Seek inspiration.

Goals for Relationships and Community

- ☐ Build a Support System: Surround yourself with a supportive community.
- ☐ Give Back: Contribute positively.
- ☐ Share Your "Toys": Be generous with resources.
- ☐ Forgive and Forget: Let go of grudges.
- ☐ Create a "Pack" Mentality: Foster unity in relationships.
- ☐ Be Loyal: Stand by loved ones.
- ☐ Celebrate Others' Success: Cheer for others' achievements.
- ☐ Offer a Helping Paw: Support those in need.
- ☐ Practice Inclusion: Include everyone.
- ☐ Stay Playful in Relationships: Keep interactions fun.
- ☐ Be a Good Listener: Listen empathetically.
- ☐ Collaborate, Don't Compete: Work together.
- ☐ Share Your Tricks: Share knowledge generously.
- ☐ Create Harmony: Strive for balance.
- ☐ Show Appreciation: Express gratitude.
- ☐ Practice Generosity: Give freely.
- ☐ Value Diversity: Embrace different perspectives.
- ☐ Build Trust: Earn trust through honesty.
- ☐ Stand Up for Others: Advocate for fairness.
- ☐ Be Present in Relationships: Engage fully.

Pawsitivity Unleashed

Goals for Productivity and Success

- ☐ Bounce Back: Recover from setbacks.
- ☐ Find the Silver Lining: See positives in challenges.
- ☐ Learn from Challenges: Grow from difficulties.
- ☐ Adopt a Growth Mindset: Believe in growth.
- ☐ Stay Adaptable: Adjust to changes.
- ☐ Lean on Your Pack: Seek support.
- ☐ Stay Grounded in Storms: Find inner strength.
- ☐ Maintain Hope: Believe in brighter days.
- ☐ Do not Bark Up the Wrong Tree: Focus on solutions.
- ☐ Channel Your Inner Doggedness: Be determined.
- ☐ Weather Life's Seasons: Adapt to life's changes.
- ☐ Build Emotional Resilience: Strengthen emotional strength.
- ☐ View Challenges as Training: See challenges as growth opportunities.
- ☐ Stay Centered in Chaos: Keep calm in turmoil.
- ☐ Cultivate Inner Strength: Grow inner resilience.
- ☐ Seek Guidance: Learn from mentors.
- ☐ Accept Impermanence: Embrace change.
- ☐ Stay Persistent: Keep moving forward.
- ☐ Practice Self-Compassion in Tough Times: Be kind to yourself.
- ☐ Know When to Rest: Listen to your needs.

Pawsitivity Unleashed

Goals for Resilience and Coping

- ☐ Bounce Back: Recover from setbacks.
- ☐ Find the Silver Lining: See positives in challenges.
- ☐ Learn from Challenges: Grow from difficulties.
- ☐ Adopt a Growth Mindset: Believe in growth.
- ☐ Stay Adaptable: Adjust to changes.
- ☐ Lean on Your Pack: Seek support.
- ☐ Stay Grounded in Storms: Find inner strength.
- ☐ Maintain Hope: Believe in brighter days.
- ☐ Do not Bark Up the Wrong Tree: Focus on solutions.
- ☐ Channel Your Inner Doggedness: Be determined.
- ☐ Weather Life's Seasons: Adapt to life's changes.
- ☐ Build Emotional Resilience: Strengthen emotional strength.
- ☐ View Challenges as Training: See challenges as growth opportunities.
- ☐ Stay Centered in Chaos: Keep calm in turmoil.
- ☐ Cultivate Inner Strength: Grow inner resilience.
- ☐ Seek Guidance: Learn from mentors.
- ☐ Accept Impermanence: Embrace change.
- ☐ Stay Persistent: Keep moving forward.
- ☐ Practice Self-Compassion in Tough Times: Be kind to yourself.
- ☐ Know When to Rest: Listen to your needs.

Goals for Health and Well-being

- [ ] Physical Exercise: Regular exercise improves overall health.
- [ ] Healthy Diet: What you consume affects your well-being.
- [ ] Rest: Adequate rest is vital for a productive life.
- [ ] Hydration: Drink enough water for optimal health.
- [ ] Sunshine: Sunlight boosts mood and provides Vitamin D.
- [ ] Mental Stimulation: Keep your mind active to stay sharp.
- [ ] Laughter: Laughter is good medicine for the soul.
- [ ] Gratitude Journaling: Writing down what you are thankful for promotes positivity.
- [ ] Meditation: Meditation calms the mind and reduces stress.
- [ ] Disconnecting: Taking breaks from screens is good for mental health.

Goals for Financial Management

- ☐ Budgeting: Knowing where your money goes leads to financial stability.
- ☐ Saving: Saving for the future provides security.
- ☐ Investing: Putting money to work grows wealth.
- ☐ Delayed Gratification: Patience with spending leads to better rewards.
- ☐ Financial Education: Continually learn about managing money.
- ☐ Emergency Fund: Having a safety net reduces stress.
- ☐ Avoiding Debt: Living within your means prevents financial strain.
- ☐ Charity: Giving back to others enriches the soul.
- ☐ Financial Goals: Clear financial goals lead to better planning.
- ☐ Seeking Advice: Consulting experts help in making wise financial decisions.

Goals for Personal Development

- ☐ Travel: Travel broadens perspectives and enriches experiences.
- ☐ Volunteering: Giving time to others brings fulfillment.
- ☐ Reading: Reading expands knowledge and understanding.
- ☐ Hobbies: Pursuing hobbies adds joy and balance to life.
- ☐ Learning a Skill: Constantly learning keeps the mind sharp.
- ☐ Journaling: Writing thoughts down clarifies emotions.
- ☐ Cultural Exploration: Learning about other cultures fosters understanding.
- ☐ Public Speaking: Overcoming fear of public speaking builds confidence.
- ☐ Networking Events: Meeting new people opens doors.
- ☐ Teaching: Teaching others reinforces your own knowledge.

Goals for Creativity and Innovation

- ☐ Brainstorming: Generating ideas freely leads to innovation.
- ☐ Experimentation: Trying new things fosters creativity.
- ☐ Inspiration Boards: Creating visual representations of goals motivates.
- ☐ Collaboration: Working with others sparks creativity.
- ☐ Feedback: Seeking feedback improves ideas.
- ☐ Iterative Improvement: Constantly refining ideas leads to excellence.
- ☐ Divergent Thinking: Thinking outside the norm generates unique solutions.
- ☐ Cross-Training: Learning from different fields sparks innovation.
- ☐ Open-Mindedness: Being open to innovative ideas breeds creativity.
- ☐ Playfulness: Approaching tasks with playfulness sparks creativity.

Goals for Leadership and Influence

- ☐ Leading by Example: Actions speak louder than words.
- ☐ Effective Communication: Clear communication avoids misunderstandings.
- ☐ Empowerment: Empowering others fosters growth.
- ☐ Problem Solving: Addressing issues directly prevents escalation.
- ☐ Vision: Having an unobstructed vision inspires others.
- ☐ Inspiration: Inspiring others creates motivated teams.
- ☐ Decision-Making: Decisiveness leads to progress.
- ☐ Conflict Resolution: Handling conflicts constructively promotes harmony.

4

Chapter Four

My Unraveling & Turning Point for Change

A Journey of Mindset & Approach

As I sit down to reflect on the twists and turns of my life, I am reminded that our journey often takes unexpected paths, leading us to places we never imagined. Over the last fourteen years, I have collaborated extensively with canines, whether it be for training, professional breeding of standard poodles for American Kennel Club dog shows, support animals or health-tested family pets. Eight years ago, I married a resolute Navy Chief, and together we shared the joys and challenges of raising four children - my son and my three stepchildren.

Life in the military is a unique and demanding experience, not just for the service member but also for the spouse. The challenges faced by women in the military as wives and mothers are both shared and deeply personal. My husband's frequent deployments turned my world upside down, and I found myself navigating the complexities of being a full-time mother and all the worries of my husband away on missions on active duty.

The transition from a full-time career to a stay-at-home mother brought about a profound shift in my identity. I had to reevaluate my entire thought system, questioning who I was and what defined me. For so long, my career had been a significant part of my identity, and suddenly, I was thrust into the role of a full-time mother, a role I had not envisioned for myself.

Deployments became routine in our lives, and I faced the challenge of raising four children on my own. Living in a place where I knew no one, with family miles away, I grappled with a sense of isolation. It was during these moments that I truly began to discover the strength within myself.

Before entering this phase of my life, I emerged from a challenging relationship that left me feeling broken and doubting my self-worth. Recovery from that relationship took a long time, but it was during this period that I met my incredible husband. Together, we faced life's complexities, supporting each other through difficulties, insecurities, and fears.

Pawsitivity Unleashed

The strength of a relationship is truly evaluated in times of adversity, and my husband and I encountered our fair share. It is not about finding perfection in a partner; it is about finding someone willing to work through imperfections and challenges together. Building strong relationships takes time and patience. I feel truly fortunate to have crossed paths with my husband. We may not have been "perfect" when we first met, but we were two people who loved and respected each other, understanding that any relationship requires time, patience, and a shared commitment to weather life's storms. Today, he is my perfect match. Sometimes, blessings come into our lives before we even realize we need them or know what to do with them. However, when we keep our head and heart in the right place and do the right things, blessings eventually find their way to us.

As my husband approached the end of his twenty-one years in the military and started his transition into retirement, a new chapter began for me as well. I was approaching forty, and I felt a deep longing for a new adventure beyond being a stay-at-home mom and military spouse. With my husband's unwavering support, I started to rediscover some of my passions – writing, dog training with Heidi, spending time outdoors, reading, and prioritizing my health and wellness. It felt invigorating. I had long neglected myself. I had prioritized everyone else and dismissed many of my needs, focusing on raising the children. Doctors began to note I needed to make changes too, and I knew I wanted to do better for my children. Even if I could not find the motivation to do it for myself, at least work on it so that my children understood how important it is to have self-care and take care of yourself. So that is what I did.

I began to make small changes, which turned into more significant changes to my diet. I increased my physical activity slowly and started finding activities I enjoyed, walks, runs with the dogs. It started with a mile a day, then two, three, up to five a day. I would play my favorite motivational tracks and music and go. In total I lost eighty pounds. This transformation opened my eyes to the importance of health for myself, my family, and our furry companions.

At the same time, I noticed that my dogs' health could be improved too. The "poodle crew" of seven were all healthy but I noticed two girls were showing signs of some allergy issues, and Heidi's joint issues crept up. She was now nine and lead grandma of the house, survived getting hit but a car before I adopted her, and has epilepsy. She is a trooper, but she was having a good amount of pain. Despite searching for the right supplements to alleviate her hip pain, I struggled to find a product with the purity and potency I desired. Frustrated by the additives and fillers in many options, I decided to create my own. After thorough research and collaboration with manufacturers and canine nutritionists, I developed Pawsitivity – a line of natural nutritional supplements for dogs.

I started with BoneBounce, our product that supports joint health, while ZenBlend addresses Heidi's anxiety during thunderstorms. Both are made with high-quality natural ingredients and free from unnecessary additives. These products are available in powder form for easy administration and can be added to meals or homemade treats. I wanted to make sure it was not a chew, because I saw the amount of product that went into it was unnecessary. With Heidi, limiting anything that was not natural was vital. She has had seizures in the past from vaccinations, stress, foods etc. so I had placed her on a limited diet, tracked her vaccinations and since she has been seizure free for the last five years. I started there and went on to create products to benefit our babies we breed and our adults that are our family pets. From treat toppers, to goat milk to pumpkin powder all natural. They loved it. They have tried them all.

They got so into it that Ginger and Ruby our two red standard poodle girls started their own YouTube Cooking show, and we made their first Pet Cookbook for dogs and Cats featuring Pawsitivity recipes taste tested by the crew. Today, Heidi is thriving with the natural supplements tailored to her unique needs, and I am proud to share Pawsitivity with other pet owners seeking premium, natural solutions for their beloved companions.

Pawsitivity Unleashed

The building of my passion for animals, training, and pet health and wellness commenced. It was a process of rediscovering my loves and interests, creating a path to a fulfilling and purpose-driven life. This newest journey in my life taught me the importance of resilience, the power of self-discovery, and the beauty of reinvention. It has been the biggest and most pivotal change in my life, and that is why I am so excited to share how I did it with you.

A Journey of Self Development & Growth

Life is an ongoing journey of growth, learning, and self-discovery. As I share my story, I hope to inspire you and others to embrace their own journeys, helping you to find your strength in the face of challenges and courage to reinvent yourself whenever you want. So, the adventure continues, and I eagerly anticipate the chapters that have yet to unfold.

Reflecting on the last five to eight years of my life, it is astounding to see the transformation from a stay-at-home parent to a successful CEO, philanthropist, and mother of four. Life has a way of surprising us, and my journey has been no exception. At the beginning of this period, I began my journey establishing a non-profit, Big Hugs for Little Hearts, with a vision to help children affected by trauma in 2019.

As a stay-at-home parent with four children, all under the age of ten, life was a whirlwind of diapers, playdates, and bedtime stories. While my dream of making a difference in the lives of traumatized children was taking shape, the challenges of raising a blended family presented a separate set of hurdles. Blending three boys and a girl, each at varying stages of childhood, brought forth a unique set of joys and complexities.

Five to eight years ago, my husband was actively serving in the military. The dynamics of my life were hectic, marked by the constant juggling act of raising four children, managing the intricacies of a blended family, and navigating the complexities of military life. It was during this time that I could never have imagined the profound changes that lay ahead.

Being a stay-at-home parent means being deeply invested in your children's lives. From the struggles in school to their interactions with peers, it is a journey that often becomes intertwined with our own identity. It is easy to bear the weight of their challenges as if they were our own, especially when societal pressures make us believe that we are solely responsible for their successes and failures.

My children's hardships, whether in school or personal relationships, became my own burdens to bear. The younger years were particularly challenging as I internalized their setbacks and blamed myself as a mother. A mother's innate desire for the best

Pawsitivity Unleashed

possible life for her child can often lead to self-blame when faced with difficulties.

The world has undergone significant changes since the days when children could freely roam outdoors until the streetlights illuminated the night. In my generation, outdoor play was the norm – we spent our days exploring nature, riding bikes, and creating adventures. Back then, dial-up internet and corded phones were all that we knew and missing a TV show meant waiting until next week for another chance. Today, however, parents face increased pressure to be actively involved in their children's lives, both in education and personal matters, driven by safety concerns and societal changes.

In the past three decades, families have become more guarded, wary of potential dangers lurking in society. Tragic events like the school shooting in Newtown, Connecticut, shattered the illusion of safety even in small towns. Personally, witnessing such devastation prompted me to become a more vigilant parent, especially as my son was only three at the time. Later, relocating to Charleston, South Carolina, presented new challenges in navigating the safety concerns of a larger city.

Today, the fear of sending our children to school without certainty of their return home is a harsh reality. In just one year at my children's school, we faced multiple bomb scares, assaults, and incidents involving firearms on the premises. The urgency to protect

Pawsitivity Unleashed

my children led to drastic measures, including transferring them to safer schools and considering private education options for added safety assurance.

In the face of these challenges, I came to realize the profound importance of taking meaningful action. Diving into research and examining the statistics, I uncovered a troubling reality. In South Carolina alone, between 2018 and 2019, there were 1.1 million reported cases of maltreatment toward children under the age of 18 (Hearts, 2024). These cases ranged from neglect in various forms, including educational and medical neglect, to more severe forms such as physical, sexual, and emotional abuse.

Child maltreatment is a deeply concerning issue that impacts the lives of countless children nationwide. However, amidst this distressing reality, there is hope. I discovered that many of these cases were rooted in families facing financial hardships, often lacking the resources needed for necessities like food, clothing, and school supplies. Additionally, many of these families grappled with mental health challenges and unresolved trauma from their own experiences of neglect and maltreatment during childhood.

This realization served as the catalyst for the creation of Big Hugs for Little Hearts. Inspired by Mahatma Gandhi's words, "Be the change you want to see in the world," our organization is committed to actively addressing the issue of child maltreatment through education, awareness, resources, support, and advocacy.

Pawsitivity Unleashed

Our mission is to engage the public and provide opportunities to prevent child abuse, neglect, and abandonment, reflecting our unwavering dedication to safeguarding the well-being of children.

Starting and running a non-profit taught me invaluable lessons about resilience, determination, and the impact of making a difference. Operating without funds and products to sell, non-profits demand a unique set of skills, yet the potential to change a child's life makes every hurdle worthwhile.

Starting a non-profit is like starting a business, but with the added challenge of additional financial constraints and the hope that people will donate to your cause. It is a journey that requires unwavering commitment, resilience, and the belief that changing even one child's life justifies every effort. As I look back on the remarkable impact, we have made on the lives of unknown children since 2019, I am reminded that sometimes, the most significant transformations stem from the humblest beginnings. The journey continues, and I eagerly anticipate the chapters yet to unfold.

A Journey of Resilience and Coping

The Importance of Never Give Up, ever!

Who could have predicted that the events of the past forty years would converge to bring me to this moment, a moment where fulfillment, happiness, and success define my life? It is often said that when you are in the thick of challenges, the light at the end of the tunnel can seem elusive.

Over the last seven to eight years, my husband and I faced some of the most significant hurdles, some we never saw coming, and others we never thought we would have to confront.

Life's trials, those moments that push us to our limits, can often feel unending. They seem unjust, nonsensical, and unrelenting, leaving us feeling disoriented and overwhelmed. But here is a promise I can offer they do end, and new chapters emerge in their wake. Even before one door closes, new beginnings wait for those who remain open to them. It is a truth I wish to impart to anyone reading this – hold on, even in the darkest and most trying of times. Stay resilient, for this too shall pass. It may seem insurmountable now, but whatever it is, it will eventually resolve. And if you believe it is beyond repair, that is okay too. It was not meant to be fixed. There is always a new path waiting to be discovered, even if

Pawsitivity Unleashed

you cannot see it yet. When one chapter ends, another begins. Always. Never lose hope! Never give up!

Overcoming the Metaphorical "The Dark Cloud"

If you have not experienced this, I am sure you most certainly will at some point in your life. The metaphorical "dark cloud" that seems to loom over our lives, bringing relentless challenges and hardships? It can feel like an endless cycle of bad luck, assessing our patience and resilience? I have had my share of encounters with that cloud, especially in 2013, just a year after giving birth to my son. The physical toll of childbirth, combined with the responsibilities of single motherhood, made those early years particularly demanding and intense. Late nights, minimal sleep, and the constant juggle between work and parenting took a toll on my well-being, yet raising my son was undeniably the greatest blessing I could have ever imagined.

Motherhood, especially as a single parent, comes with its own set of overwhelming expectations. Being the eldest child in my family, I felt the pressure to meet impossibly ambitious standards and never falter, adding to the burden of raising a child alone. Despite the challenges, I often forgot to extend myself the same grace I readily offered others.

The decision to end my engagement to my son's father and raise my son alone was a difficult one, but I knew it was the right choice for both of us. It meant facing a more challenging road ahead, but I was determined to provide my son with the best possible upbringing, even if it meant sacrificing my own comfort.

Balancing work and motherhood were another hurdle. Sick days, childcare arrangements, and the pressure to appear competent at work while dealing with personal challenges took their toll on me. I focused solely on providing for my son, neglecting my own well-being in the process. It was pure survival mode at that point. The lack of support from my ex-fiancé for the sole purpose of making it more difficult for me, gave me that much more of an incentive to thrive. I saw my mother, one of the strongest women succeed against something quite similar, and because of her strength and I will overcome this too. Often, we do not know why we go through difficult moments and sometimes we wish we had not, however after all the years pass and the dust settles, I look back and realize the biggest hurdles turn out to be the exact hurdles that guided me to my true purpose.

This was a defining period of my life, which shaped my perception of the world, my priorities, and the kind of future I saw for myself. Now, at the time I could have become complacent, discouraged, and given up. But I found something that made me push harder, I found my own . You cannot control what other people do, but you can only control how you manage what you receive. I vowed to give my son a better life and for him to not experience the struggles because I was a single mother. I worked twice as hard to make up for the void his father chose to give his son by not showing up and stepping out because it was too hard for him to see me.

My story is so common, and unfortunate for so many children. At that time, 15,000 families were single mothers in 2012-2017. The numbers have not wavered much either. According to census.gov in 2022 15,040 families were single mothers in the united state which was 80% on the single families at the time. (Census.gov, 2022) According to the Census Bureau released in November 2022 for the same time, there were 10.0 million one parent family groups with a child under the age of eighteen at the time. It also showed according to the America's Families and Living Arrangements that 80% of the one-parent family groups was maintained by a mother (Census.gov, 2022) which has truly become an epidemic for women forced to raise fatherless children. Not to say that there are no exceptions, it has just been the majority.

Every challenge, every experience, brings us closer to our true purpose. This book serves as a moment of reflection, inviting you to ponder the strengths and characteristics that brought you to this point in your own life. As you continue this 30-day journey with "Pawsitivity Unleashed," you will explore the transformative power of self-discovery and reinvention. The daily exercises, quotes, and reflections are tools borrowed from my own journey and shared with you to aid in your quest for purpose and fulfill-ment.

So, as you immerse yourself in the exercises, embrace the op-portunity to dive deep into your own journey of self-discovery. In thirty days, reevaluate yourself, rediscover your passions, and let the transformative power of introspection guide you toward a more meaningful life.

5

Chapter Five

The Unlikely Catalyst

A Process of Self-Exploration & Transformation

In the intricate fabric of life, a catalyst often emerges as the pivotal force reshaping our stories, driving us towards profound change. It could be an extraordinary event, a moment of realization, or a powerful force that sets off a chain reaction, altering our perspectives, behaviors, and circumstances. As I was beginning a journey towards significant transformation, little did I realize that the catalyst for change was already in motion. Unbeknownst to me, it would come in the form of an unlikely source: a forty-five-pound curly-haired ball of fluff whom I had yet to meet.

Let's journey back to the year 2015, when my son Ryan was just three years old. I found myself navigating the complexities of single motherhood, striving to find balance amidst the demands of a challenging job, lengthy commutes, and the lingering shadows of a past abusive relationship. Despite the trials, Ryan's love became my beacon of hope and resilience. His innocent smile and infectious laughter illuminated even the darkest days, reminding me of life's simple joys.

Single-handedly shouldering the financial responsibilities of running a household, coupled with the worries of ensuring my son's well-being and happiness without the presence of a partner, weighed heavily on my heart. While children may not grasp the complexities of their circumstances, as parents, we bear the weight of our past choices and strive to shield them from the repercussions.

I was determined not to let my son suffer for the mistakes of my past relationship. Yet, despite our best efforts to shield our children, we realize that our actions may only offer partial protection. So, we do what we can, striving to provide love, support, and stability amidst life's uncertainties.

Single motherhood, for me, was burdened with lofty expectations and an unyielding quest for perfection, particularly amidst personal turmoil. I tirelessly strived to provide for my son while grappling with the challenge of holding his father accountable and supportive. Each stride I took forward seemed to be met with resistance, leaving me disheartened and depleted.

Despite my fervent desire to co-parent amicably for the sake of my son, my efforts were often in vain. I relentlessly tried to involve his father in his life, sometimes at my own expense. I was willing to sacrifice my well-being in the hope that Ryan wouldn't have to navigate life without his father's presence. However, my endeavors proved futile, leaving me shattered and Ryan fatherless.

Faced with disappointment, I turned inward, redirecting my focus solely on my son. Determined to provide him with stability and love, I resolved to navigate parenthood alone, shielding him from the unpredictable presence of his father, who would sporadically appear only to disappear when his desires were unmet.

Amidst the chaos of that period, I made a deliberate effort to infuse our home with love. Drawing upon my lifelong affinity for dogs, I welcomed Heidi, a black Standard Poodle, into our lives. Despite Heidi's tumultuous journey – surviving a car accident, battling early onset seizures, and grappling with anxiety before the age of two – I remained undeterred. My childhood fondness for poodles, coupled with my knowledge of canine health and wellness and experience as a dog trainer, equipped me to care for her. I diligently managed her seizures and administered her daily medication.

Pawsitivity Unleashed

Whether Heidi's epilepsy stemmed from the accident, or a vaccination remained uncertain, but I was unwavering in my commitment to her well-being. I immersed myself in researching and caring for her, determined to provide her with the best possible care. Little did I anticipate that Heidi would not only bring warmth and joy into our home but also ignite a profound journey of self-discovery within myself.

Heidi bounded into our home, radiating vitality and joy despite her struggles with seizures. From the start, her obsession with tennis balls and bouts of anxiety were evident. Her exuberant barking, urging us to play, hinted at a deeper restlessness beneath the surface. Initially, I dismissed it as typical dog behavior, but upon closer observation, it became clear that her behavior was more than just enthusiasm – it was driven by anxiety and obsession.

To address Heidi's needs, I implemented a two-pronged approach. First, I ensured she received ample exercise to burn off excess energy, while also cultivating a serene atmosphere indoors. Sensitivity to loud noises prompted the use of a sound machine and air filter to create a calm environment. During the day, soothing Disney movies played in the background, providing comfort and reassurance. With only Ryan and me in the household, Heidi enjoyed undivided attention and the freedom to roam.

Treating her like royalty, Heidi luxuriated in a comfortable environment, complete with blankets, pillows, and plush beds fit for

Pawsitivity Unleashed

a princess. Transitioning to a natural diet and reducing stress further alleviated her anxiety symptoms. However, my initial encounter with one of Heidi's seizures was deeply emotional. It occurred shortly after her adoption, catching me off guard and leaving me feeling helpless as I watched her experience the seizure.

In those tense moments, I remained by her side, offering comfort and reassurance until the seizure subsided. Afterward, a soothing bath and tender care helped her recover, but the fear of another episode lingered. Consulting with a veterinarian, we discussed treatment options and secured backup medications as a precautionary measure.

Through a combination of dietary changes, stress reduction techniques, and increased exercise, Heidi's seizures gradually became less frequent. Today, I'm grateful to say that Heidi has been seizure-free for over five years, a testament to the power of patience, love, and dedication in overcoming adversity.

Heidi's journey with epilepsy and anxiety served as a catalyst for positive change, not only in her life but also in mine. Witnessing her resilience ignited a newfound interest in nutrition, exercise, and holistic well-being. With Heidi as our faithful companion, our family embarked on a transformative journey towards improved health and overall well-being.

Pawsitivity Unleashed

We embraced a more active lifestyle, spending quality time outdoors and indulging in simple pleasures like playing fetch with tennis balls – Heidi's absolute favorite pastime. Her gentle demeanor endeared her to my son, who delighted in her playful and endearing antics. As she seamlessly integrated into our home, her presence brought boundless joy and stability, particularly during significant family milestones.

From the moment I met my now-husband, through our wedding and subsequent relocation to Charleston, South Carolina, Heidi remained a constant source of comfort and companionship. Whether accompanying us on long drives or settling into the front seat for a car ride, her enthusiasm for adventure and love for car rides never wavered. Her presence made every journey enjoyable, especially for Ryan, who cherished their shared moments together.

When Your Catalyst Initiates Change

Heidi's arrival sparked a profound shift within me, compelling me to venture beyond my comfort zone and reconsider my life's trajectory. In her unwavering love and loyalty, I found a mirror reflecting my own worth, prompting me to reevaluate my value to myself and to others. Amidst my struggles, Heidi's unconditional love and steadfast presence became a source of solace and inspiration.

At a time when I felt beaten down and overlooked, Heidi's devotion reminded me of my inherent value and purpose beyond conventional roles. Her daily companionship, amidst her own challenges, served as a beacon of strength, instilling in me the courage to rebuild and reinvest in myself. Like filling in the gaps with cement to fortify a foundation, her presence provided the support and reassurance I needed to navigate the uncertainties ahead.

With Heidi by my side, I gained confidence in my decisions and found solace in the knowledge that I was on the right path. Together, we faced life's challenges as a united front, laying the groundwork for personal and professional growth. Her transformative influence became the cornerstone of my journey towards self-discovery and empowerment.

When your Catalyst Builds Inspiration and Motivation

Witnessing Heidi's unwavering resilience and loyalty sparked a newfound determination within me to pursue passions and aspirations that had long been dormant. Amidst the chaos of daily struggles, I had lost sight of my own dreams, consumed by the relentless demands of life's battles. Juggling the responsibilities of single parenthood, work, finances, and myriad challenges, I found myself in survival mode, with little time or energy to focus on myself.

Yet, in the presence of Heidi and my son Ryan, a sense of tranquility enveloped me, allowing buried dreams to resurface. Heidi's companionship tapped into a creative wellspring that had lain dormant within me for too long. Together, we found solace and freedom in moments spent without care or concern.

These long-neglected dreams held profound significance, hinting at untapped potential and opportunities for growth. I realized that stifling them was not an option; they were the seeds of personal evolution waiting to be nurtured. It was time to breathe life into these aspirations, to find a way to manifest them into reality.

Revisiting these long-dormant dreams reignited a fire within me, driving me to seize control and reshape not only my own life but also the future of my family. With renewed determination, I set out to unlock doors that had long remained closed, embarking on a journey to fulfill these deeply cherished aspirations.

The Realization of Your Own Potential

From Heidi's perspective, I was already a shining star – someone amazing, fun, and her closest companion. Her unwavering trust and loyalty empowered me in ways she may never have realized. This is the enchantment of our bond with dogs – it transcends words, fostering profound connections rooted in intuition and understanding. Dogs possess a remarkable ability to perceive the essence of people, recognizing hidden greatness where others may not. Heidi saw my potential long before I did, serving as a steadfast source of encouragement and inspiration.

Sometimes, it takes someone else's belief in you to ignite your own belief in yourself. There are moments when we doubt our own abilities, and we need a gentle reminder or a nudge from a special individual – a little angel– to reaffirm our worth. For me, that special someone was Heidi.

Breaking Patterns to Create Something Better

When Heidi entered our lives, it necessitated a reevaluation of our family's daily routines. As a new member of the household, we had to ensure she received proper care – walks during the day, regular feeding times, and sufficient exercise. Adapting to these changes meant breaking old patterns and forming new habits, which initially proved challenging and frustrating. However, as consistency set in, these adjustments became routine and effortless. Yet, falling into a routine can lead to complacency, where we stop actively participating in our own lives.

Have you ever found yourself driving to work, lost in music or thoughts, only to realize you missed your turn? Your brain was on autopilot, guiding you down familiar paths without conscious thought. Similarly, falling into predictable patterns can lead to feeling unfulfilled and frustrated because we stop actively engaging with our surroundings.

Pawsitivity Unleashed

Heidi's health challenges prompted a shift in our mindset and routines, encouraging us to think differently and embrace change. As I navigated her seizures, I discovered newfound resilience and resourcefulness, drawing upon my knowledge of canine health and wellness to provide her with the best care possible. Implementing dietary changes and stress reduction techniques helped to manage her seizures and alleviate her anxiety, resulting in a more peaceful environment for us all.

Observing the positive impact of these changes inspired me to make similar shifts in my own life. I prioritized exercise, adopted healthier eating habits, and embraced change with open arms. The results were transformative – I began to look and feel better, shedding excess weight and gaining a newfound confidence. My skin glowed with vitality, and I rediscovered the joy of dressing up. These positive changes attracted new friends and opportunities into my life, marking the beginning of a positive transformation journey.

When Your Catalyst Encourages Self-Reflection

Heidi's journey prompted me to embark on my own path of self-reflection, leading to profound changes and progress towards my goals. Her influence compelled me to examine my values, priorities, and long-term aspirations, marking the beginning of my re-invention journey. Through introspection, I gained clarity about my desires and ambitions, laying the foundation for transformation.

Taking that initial step towards change was daunting, as I confronted my own internal resistance. Yet, overcoming these self-imposed barriers was essential. It taught me that I possessed the resilience and determination to surmount any obstacle once I overcame my inner dialogue. Breaking down my goals into manageable steps allowed me to track my progress and witness tangible results. Each small achievement became a cause for celebration, reinforcing my sense of value, strength, and worth.

Your Catalyst as Your Guide

Heidi's journey became a driving force for my personal growth and self-exploration, motivating me to welcome change and pursue my dreams with newfound determination. In her own special way, Heidi became a beacon of guidance during a pivotal phase of my life. Her presence brought fresh insights and encouraged positive shifts in my perspective. Heidi sparked transformations within me that may have remained dormant without her influence. Encounters like ours are rare but carry profound impact, shaping our paths in unexpected and meaningful ways.

Overcoming Adversity Together

I've never encountered a dog as resilient, courageous, and triumphant in the face of adversity as Heidi. Her ability to overcome challenges is nothing short of remarkable, driven by her unwavering diligence and determination. Despite enduring a severe accident that left lasting effects, Heidi persevered with remarkable resilience. In 2020, she even survived an encounter with an Eastern Copperhead, further demonstrating her incredible strength.

Throughout our journey together, we've prioritized Heidi's well-being through a natural, healthy diet, daily exercise, and stress reduction techniques. These efforts have contributed to her remarkable achievement of five years without seizures. Heidi's journey has taught me invaluable lessons about personal strength and resilience, emphasizing the importance of recognizing our strengths and recognizing our achievements.

When Your Catalyst Prompts Re-evaluation of Priorities

When Heidi entered my life, she immediately captured my heart and prompted me to reassess my priorities, prompting deep reflection on what truly mattered to me. This led me to redefine my goals and scrutinize my core values, ensuring they aligned with my life choices and what held genuine significance for me.

During moments of struggle, I discovered that my true core values, essential to my well-being, might not always be apparent in major life areas such as career, family, and friendships. Feeling unsettled often signaled a misalignment between my values and life circumstances, urging me to realign my goals and decisions with my authentic self.

From that pivotal moment onward, I instituted regular self-checks to ensure my values and aspirations remained in harmony. If discrepancies arose, I took proactive steps to adjust, whether that meant cultivating new friendships or pursuing a different career path. Recognizing the discord between my values and actions helped me avoid discontentment, and periodic assessments served as reminders to stay true to myself and take necessary action.

When Your Catalyst Sparks Creativity

As Heidi matured, she maintained the vibrant spirit of her youth, ageless until one day when I noticed her limping while playing with the other poodles. This behavior, out of character for her, raised concerns as she gradually became less active and hesitant to go outside. After allowing her to rest for a few days, I decided to take her to the vet for evaluation.

Despite Heidi's stoic demeanor, the vet recommended X-rays to rule out any serious injuries. Thankfully, no broken bones were found, but signs of muscle loss prompted the suspicion of arthritis and hip and joint pain. With pain medication prescribed, we embarked on a trial period to assess her response.

During this time, I delved into research on natural supplements to manage her discomfort, only to find limited options that met my criteria. Frustrated by the lack of suitable choices, I was inspired by Heidi's resilience to explore my creativity in new ways. Drawing upon her strength, I ventured into the creation of natural canine supplements tailored to her specific needs.

Heidi's presence ignited a newfound sense of purpose, motivating me to pursue other artistic endeavors as well including drawing, painting, and writing with newfound freedom and courage. This shift from seeking external validation to making a tangible difference in Heidi's well-being was invigorating and deeply fulfilling.

When Your Catalyst Enhances Your Well-Being

Heidi's influence transcended mere sparks of creativity, prompting a profound reevaluation of my priorities, and extending to the enhancement of my own health and well-being. Her boundless love taught me the importance of self-care and compassion, while her selfless nature demonstrated the immense rewards of giving without expectation of reciprocation. Through her example, I rediscovered my passion for helping others, reigniting a long-held dream of starting a nonprofit to support abused, abandoned, and neglected children—a dream I had harbored since the age of sixteen but had long forgotten.

As you embark on your own journey of self-discovery, let Heidi's story serve as a reminder of the transformative power that one individual—or pup—can wield in your life. Embrace new interests and opportunities, recognizing the potential for profound change. Remember Theodore Roosevelt's words, "Believe you can, and you're halfway there," and hold onto that belief as you embark on new beginnings. Explore uncharted territories, uncovering deeper insights into your passions and purpose. May you find your own catalyst for transformative change from within, leading you to the fulfillment and growth you seek.

6

Chapter Six

The Power of a Transformation Guide

My Canine Companion & Key to Transformation

Embarking on a journey of transformation frequently entails seeking guidance and support, but we often underestimate the profound impact our loyal canine companions can have during this period. Dogs possess an extraordinary ability to guide us toward personal growth and self-discovery with their unwavering loyalty, unconditional love, and innate wisdom. They hold the potential to impart invaluable life lessons, provided we approach our relationship with them with open eyes and receptive hearts.

The Power of Canine Companionship

When I invite a dog into my life, they transcend being mere pets; they become trusted companions and confidants. Their presence profoundly influences the overall well-being of myself and my family, offering comfort, companionship, and a sense of purpose. Through their unwavering loyalty and affection, they underscore the significance of connection and companionship, lifting our spirits, alleviating stress, and filling our hearts with joy.

Beyond their role as household pets, dogs possess unique qualities that make them invaluable guides for personal transformation. Their instinctual nature, keen intuition, and steadfast presence equip them to serve as powerful allies on our journey of self-discovery. By observing their behavior and learning from their example, we can glean valuable insights into our own thought patterns and behaviors. As we've observed thus far, much of how we train them, particularly when using positive reinforcement methods, reflects how we navigate our lives. Considering this, it's not far-fetched to imagine that they may have valuable lessons to teach us. Let's explore further.

The Canine Guide to Transformation

Through my personal journey of transformation, coupled with years of experience in dog training and breeding, I've discovered that our canine companions offer invaluable guidance and support.

Their simple yet profound way of being holds the power to impart important life lessons that we can apply to our own lives, particularly during times of transformation, to ignite inspirational change and momentum.

Here are some key principles I've gleaned, which proved fundamental in my own transformation and made the most significant impact when applied. These insights emerged after fourteen years of working closely with dogs, and surprisingly, upon reflection, mirrored the steps I needed to take in my own transformative journey. As such, they have become foundational life principles. While some may appear straightforward, they often present challenges when translated into real-life action.

Learning to Live in the Present Moment

Living in the present moment may seem straightforward, but it becomes challenging when we find ourselves entangled in the past. Dogs possess a remarkable innate ability to fully immerse themselves in the present, unburdened by concerns about the past or future. They don't hold grudges or dwell on events from minutes ago; instead, they focus on the beauty of each moment as it unfolds. Through their example, they teach us mindfulness and the importance of staying grounded in the here and now, letting go of regrets and anxieties.

Even in the face of severe abuse and neglect, dogs demonstrate resilience and gentleness, offering a powerful reminder of the strength found in living fully in the present moment.

While reflecting on the past can sometimes be necessary for moving forward, dwelling on it indefinitely can hinder our progress. People who remain fixated on events from decades ago often find themselves trapped in a cycle of the same thought patterns and emotions from that time. While we cannot change the past or predict the future, we do have control over the present moment. Learning to embrace the now allows us to release ourselves from the grip of "what ifs" and "could have been," enabling us to fully experience what is happening in the present.

Embracing Unconditional Love

Recognizing our inherent worthiness of love is a valuable concept that many struggle with, particularly when we perceive ourselves as imperfect or believe we could be better. We may dwell on past mistakes or harbor feelings of unworthiness, failing to realize that making mistakes is an essential part of being human. While some argue that success can also be a teacher, the depth of understanding gained from repeated failure far surpasses that of occasional success. Failure, they viewed is not something to be feared but viewed as an opportunity for growth and learning. If we glean no insight from our failures, then indeed, we have failed. However, if we extract valuable lessons from our mistakes, they become nothing more than temporary challenges.

Granting ourselves grace, or unconditional love, is crucial in this process. Dogs exemplify this unconditional love, accepting us without judgment and loving us for who we are. By practicing self-compassion and acceptance daily, we can emulate their unconditional love and cultivate deeper love and compassion for ourselves and others. Just as dogs offer unwavering love to us, so too can we offer ourselves compassion and acceptance as we navigate the journey of life.

The Importance of Cultivating Resilience

In any journey, the ability to foster resilience is crucial, as it enables you to persevere in the face of setbacks. Dogs exemplify resilience, bouncing back from challenges with unwavering determination. Those who have owned or rescued dogs can attest to this firsthand. Dogs teach us the importance of resilience and perseverance when confronting adversity. They show us how crucial it is to view challenges as opportunities for growth and to approach them with resilience. Instead of perceiving challenges as punishments or attacks, we can choose to see them as tests of our abilities and mental fortitude.

By shifting our perspective and viewing challenges as opportunities for personal growth, rather than as obstacles to overcome, we can navigate our journey with greater ease. Perspective and perception become powerful tools in cultivating resilience during difficult times.

Learning to Trust our Intuition.

One of the most invaluable lessons I've learned is to trust my intuition—a skill that dogs rely on instinctively to navigate their world. Despite their inability to speak our language, dogs communicate through body language, using subtle cues like pinned-back ears, intense stares, or frozen poses to convey their feelings and intentions to us and to other dogs. As a trainer, I've come to understand the nuanced meanings behind these behaviors, which often signal when something is amiss or when a potential threat is present.

As humans, we possess this same innate sense of intuition—a gut feeling that alerts us when something doesn't seem right or when a situation feels off. However, we often disregard our intuition, overridden by the rationalizations of our mind or the desires of our heart. Learning to trust our intuition is invaluable; it's a gift that allows us to perceive things beyond what our eyes can see, tapping into a deeper level of understanding. Often, when we ignore our intuition, we regret it later, wishing we had listened to that inner voice nudging us in the right direction.

Pawsitivity Unleashed

Dogs serve as powerful reminders to trust our instincts and inner voice, guiding us toward the right decisions and paths in life. Their unwavering trust in their intuition encourages us to do the same, reminding us that sometimes, the answers we seek lie within ourselves.

Learning to Embrace Joy and Playfulness

Dogs possess an innate ability to exude joy and playfulness, serving as constant reminders for us humans to not take life too seriously. Their infectious enthusiasm and boundless energy have a way of bringing out our inner child, prompting us to embrace spontaneity and find joy in the simplest of moments.

In a world filled with deadlines, responsibilities, and stressors, dogs encourage us to pause, breathe, and appreciate the present moment. Whether it's chasing after a ball, rolling around in the grass, or simply basking in the warmth of the sun, they remind us of the importance of living in the here and now.

By embracing their carefree spirit, we can learn to let go of unnecessary worries and anxieties, simplifying our lives and reconnecting with what truly matters. Instead of getting caught up in the hustle and bustle of everyday life, we can take a cue from our canine companions and find happiness in the simple pleasures that surround us. Whether it's the wag of a tail, the slobbery kiss of a wet nose, or the excitement of a walk in the park, dogs show us that joy can be found in even the most mundane moments.

Establishing the Unbreakable Bond: My Journey with Heidi

From the moment I embarked on my journey with Heidi, there was an immediate and profound connection. It deepened as she entrusted me to care for her, to comfort her through her first seizure, and the ones that followed. With each passing day, our relationship blossomed, fortified by trust, understanding, and shared experiences.

As she became an integral part of our family, Heidi not only welcomed my son into her heart but also embraced him as her own. Together, we navigated life's difficulties, supported each other through challenges, and celebrated moments of joy and love.

Over the years, our bond has only grown stronger, rooted in mutual respect, unwavering loyalty, and unconditional love. Through every trial and triumph, we have remained steadfast companions, knowing that we can always rely on each other.

Through my journey with Heidi, I learned the importance of nurturing and cultivating meaningful connections. By prioritizing trust, communication, and empathy, we have forged a bond that transcends words and speaks to the depths of our souls. These principles have not only enriched our lives but have also guided me on my path to personal growth and fulfillment.

Building Trust and Mutual Respect

The bond between Heidi and me began to form the instant our paths crossed. From that initial moment of connection, we embarked on a journey of mutual understanding, patience, and growth. With every interaction, we remained committed to fostering a relationship built on positive reinforcement and unwavering support.

Patience became our guiding principle as we navigated the difficulties of our journey together. We understood that true connection takes time to cultivate and that every interaction was an opportunity to strengthen our bond. Through patience, we learned to appreciate each other's unique qualities and quirks, fostering a deeper sense of connection and companionship.

Central to our relationship was the emphasis on positive reinforcement. Rather than focusing on shortcomings or mistakes, we chose to highlight and celebrate each other's successes and achievements. By consistently reinforcing positive behaviors and attitudes, we created an environment of trust, encouragement, and growth.

Trust and respect formed the bedrock of our relationship. We understood the importance of reliability and honesty in building a strong bond, and we prioritized these values in our interactions. Through open communication and mutual respect, we cultivated a deep sense of trust that allowed us to navigate challenges with confidence and resilience.

As our relationship evolved, so did our understanding of each other. We embraced our differences and celebrated our shared experiences, fostering a sense of camaraderie and mutual support. Together, we learned valuable lessons about patience, positivity, trust, and respect, laying the foundation for a lifelong bond built on love and companionship.

Navigating Challenges and Overcoming Obstacles

Throughout our journey, Heidi and I encountered numerous challenges that tested our resolve and strengthened our bond. With each obstacle we faced, we stood by each other's side, offering unwavering support and encouragement in the form of love and attention and her, companionships, and affection. These challenges became opportunities for growth, allowing us to deepen our connection and reaffirm our commitment to one another.

As we navigated setbacks and difficulties, our bond grew stronger. I learned I could lean on her for support, drawing strength from our shared experiences and unwavering determination. Together, we faced adversity with resilience and perseverance, refusing to let obstacles deter us from my path.

Pawsitivity Unleashed

In moments of doubt or uncertainty, I relied on her as a sounding board for guidance and reassurance. She was a great listener. Our mutual trust and understanding served as pillars of strength, anchoring us during times of turmoil. With every challenge we overcame, our bond deepened, solidifying our partnership and reinforcing team spirit.

Through perseverance and determination, I emerged from each obstacle stronger and more resilient than before. Our journey together became a testament to the power of companionship and the importance of facing challenges head-on. Together, I learned valuable lessons about resilience, perseverance, and the enduring power of friendship.

Embracing Vulnerability and Authenticity

My bond with Heidi transcends superficial interactions; it's rooted in vulnerability and authenticity. With her, I feel completely at ease, able to express myself authentically without fear of judgment. Heidi's unwavering acceptance and unconditional love create a safe space where I can be vulnerable and open.

In moments of joy, sadness, or uncertainty, Heidi remains a constant source of comfort and solace. Her presence alone is enough to ease any worries or anxieties, reminding me of the importance of vulnerability in our connection. Through sharing my deepest thoughts and emotions, we strengthen our bond, fostering a deeper understanding and appreciation for each other.

Heidi's ability to love unconditionally serves as a powerful reminder of the beauty of vulnerability. In her presence, I am encouraged to embrace my true self, flaws, and all, knowing that I am accepted and loved for who I am. Our relationship thrives on authenticity, creating a strong foundation built on mutual trust and understanding.

As I continue my journey with her, together, I cherish the moments of vulnerability and authenticity that strengthen our bond. Through openness and honesty, I deepen our connection, forging a relationship built on love, trust, and genuine companionship.

Celebrating Victories and Milestones

Our journey together has been filled with countless moments of celebration and triumph, each one strengthening the bond between Heidi and me. From the exhilarating drive home when I first welcomed her into our lives to the challenges we've overcome together, our connection has only grown stronger with each shared victory.

As I navigate life's difficulties, Heidi and I find joy in each other's achievements, big and small. Whether it's conquering her fears during training sessions or reaching a new milestone in her recovery, every success is cause for celebration. These shared triumphs serve as reminders of our unwavering dedication to each other and reinforce the deep bond we share.

Our journey together began with a leap of faith, and since then, we've faced numerous challenges head-on, from Heidi's first seizures to the excitement of moving homes and welcoming new companions into our lives. Through it all, Heidi has remained a steadfast source of strength and joy, her presence bringing light and warmth to even the darkest days.

As we look back on our journey so far, we're filled with gratitude for the milestones we've achieved together and the victories we've celebrated along the way. With Heidi by my side, I know that no challenge is too great, and no dream is out of reach. Together, we'll continue to conquer whatever obstacles lie ahead, fueled by the unwavering bond we share.

Nurturing the Bond through Daily Rituals

Our daily rituals and routines continue to anchor our bond. From morning walks to evening snuggles, these moments continue to strengthen our connection. Special treats and grooming sessions become cherished rituals that also add value to our relationship and deepen our bond.

Heidi's love and companionship have enriched my life in ways I never imagined. Our bond is unbreakable, offering strength and

Pawsitivity Unleashed

support through life's difficulties. I am forever grateful for her presence in my life.

The bond between humans and dogs is a profound relationship that offers invaluable lessons in love, resilience, and joy. Through their wisdom and companionship, dogs guide us on a journey of self-discovery and growth, shaping us into the best versions of ourselves. Let us embrace their teachings with gratitude and open hearts, knowing that our bond with dogs is a truly transformative experience.

7

Chapter Seven

How to Set Yourself Up for Success

A Positive Mindset, Self-Development, & Resilience

When embarking on the journey towards success, it's essential to recognize that it's not just about reaching external milestones; it's a profound voyage of self-discovery, growth, and triumph over obstacles. In my own pursuit of success, I've come to understand that it's the combination of mindset, ongoing self-improvement, and resilience that paves the way forward. Let's delve deeper into how these elements have influenced and guided my journey towards success.

Success isn't solely about accomplishing goals; it's a holistic journey that encompasses personal growth, self-awareness, and the ability to overcome adversity. As I reflect on my own path, I've learned that cultivating a positive mindset is paramount. It's about adopting a mentality of abundance, resilience, and unwavering determination. This mindset shift has allowed me to approach challenges with a sense of optimism and possibility, propelling me forward even in the face of setbacks.

Moreover, continuous self-development has been instrumental in my journey towards success. It involves a commitment to lifelong learning, self-reflection, and personal growth. By investing in my own development through reading, attending workshops, and seeking mentorship, I've been able to expand my knowledge, skills, and perspectives. This continuous evolution has not only enhanced my capabilities but has also empowered me to adapt to changing circumstances and seize new opportunities.

Additionally, resilience has been a cornerstone of my success journey. It's the ability to bounce back from setbacks, learn from failures, and persevere in the face of adversity. Resilience isn't about avoiding challenges; it's about embracing them as opportunities for growth and learning. Through resilience, I've discovered my inner strength and capacity to overcome even the most daunting obstacles. It's through resilience that I've transformed setbacks into steppingstones towards success.

Pawsitivity Unleashed

Success is a multifaceted journey that requires a combination of mindset, continuous self-development, and resilience. By embracing these principles, I've been able to chart my path towards success, navigating challenges with grace and determination. Let's dive into each a little more.

The Power of a Positive Mindset

The concept of mindset transcends mere thoughts; it serves as a powerful filter that shapes our perceptions, responses, and our outcomes in life. In the initial stages of my journey, I became acutely aware of the profound influence of mindset on every facet of my existence. It became evident to me that the lens through which we view the world significantly impacts how we navigate challenges, pursue our aspirations, and interpret our experiences.

Diving deeper into the meaning of mindset, I uncovered its transformative potential. I realized that by adopting a positive and growth-oriented mindset, I could unlock new realms of possibility and propel myself towards success. It was a realization that fundamentally altered the trajectory of my journey. As I cultivated a mindset rooted in optimism, resilience, and possibility, I began to witness a remarkable shift in my reality.

One of the most profound lessons I learned along the way was the principle of the Law of Attraction. It was a concept that resonated deeply with me and illuminated the interconnectedness between my thoughts, beliefs, and outcomes. I discovered that the energy I projected into the universe had a direct correlation with the experiences and opportunities that manifested in my life. By harnessing the power of positivity and focusing my thoughts on abundance and gratitude, I found myself attracting more favorable circumstances and outcomes.

Conversely, I recognized the detrimental effects of dwelling on negativity and limiting beliefs. I observed how a pessimistic mind-set could act as a barrier to progress, stifling growth and hindering my ability to seize opportunities. It was a profound revelation that underscored the importance of consciously choosing my thoughts and beliefs to align with my goals and aspirations.

Mindset emerged as a cornerstone of my journey towards success. It was not merely a passive aspect of my being but a dynamic force that shaped my reality. By embracing a positive and growth-oriented mindset, I was able to cultivate a fertile ground for success to flourish. Through the lens of mindset, I discovered the power of intentionality, resilience, and the innate capacity within each of us to shape our destinies.

How to Embrace a Growth Mindset

In addition to cultivating a positive mindset, I dove into the profound concept of the growth mindset, a principle popularized by psychologist Carol Dweck. This transformative mindset revolves around the belief that our abilities and intelligence are not fixed traits but can be developed through dedication, effort, and perseverance. It represents a change in thinking from viewing challenges as insurmountable barriers to recognizing them as opportunities for growth and self-improvement.

As I embraced the tenets of the growth mindset, I internalized the empowering notion that setbacks and challenges were not indicative of my limitations but rather steppingstones on the path to success. Each obstacle became an invitation to stretch beyond my comfort zone, acquire new skills, and refine existing ones. Instead of succumbing to feelings of defeat or inadequacy, I approached challenges with a sense of curiosity and resilience, eager to uncover the lessons they held.

For instance, when confronted with a daunting project at work, I reframed my perspective, viewing it not as an overwhelming task but as a platform for personal and professional development. Rather than allowing fear or doubt to paralyze me, I embraced the opportunity to learn, grow, and evolve. This shift in mindset propelled me forward, igniting a newfound sense of motivation and determination to surmount obstacles and achieve my goals.

The growth mindset became a guiding philosophy in my journey towards success, instilling in me the belief that with dedication, perseverance, and a willingness to embrace challenges, I could continuously expand my capabilities and reach new heights of achievement. It empowered me to approach life with a sense of optimism and possibility, viewing setbacks not as failures but as opportunities for growth and self-discovery. Through the lens of the growth mindset, every challenge became a steppingstone towards realizing my full potential.

How to Overcome Limiting Beliefs

One of the most significant hurdles I encountered on my journey to success was grappling with and overcoming limiting beliefs. These deeply ingrained beliefs, often rooted in childhood or past experiences, can exert a powerful influence on our thoughts, actions, and our outcomes. They serve as invisible barriers that hinder our progress and impede our ability to realize our full potential.

Addressing these limiting beliefs required a deliberate and concerted effort to challenge and reframe my mindset. It demanded introspection, self-awareness, and a willingness to confront the negative narratives that had been holding me back. I recognized that these beliefs, such as "I'm not good enough" or "I don't deserve success," were nothing more than self-imposed constraints that were sabotaging my growth and limiting my possibilities.

Through a process of introspection and reflection, I began to disentangle myself from these self-limiting beliefs. I acknowledged their presence and their impact on my life, but I refused to allow them to dictate my future. Instead, I embarked on a journey of self-transformation, replacing these disempowering beliefs with empowering affirmations that affirmed my worth and potential.

For example, I consciously replaced the belief "I'm not good enough" with the affirmation "I am capable and deserving of success." This simple yet profound shift in mindset served as a catalyst for change, empowering me to break free from the shackles of self-doubt and insecurity. It allowed me to step into my power and embrace my inherent worthiness, opening doors to new opportunities and possibilities that were previously beyond my reach.

By challenging and reframing my limiting beliefs, I liberated myself from the constraints of my past and paved the way for a future filled with boundless potential and limitless possibilities. This transformative journey taught me that the power to shape my destiny lies within me, and by harnessing the power of my mind, I can overcome any obstacle and achieve my dreams.

Pawsitivity Unleashed

A Journey to Self-Development & Growth

Embarking on the path to success entails more than just achieving external milestones; it encompasses a profound journey of self-discovery and personal growth. Recognizing this, I dedicated myself wholeheartedly to the pursuit of continuous learning, self-improvement, and the exploration of new horizons.

From the outset, I understood that success was not merely a destination to be reached but a dynamic process of evolution and transformation. It required a willingness to step outside my comfort zone, challenge my existing beliefs and assumptions, and embrace the discomfort of growth. Every experience, whether positive or negative, presented an opportunity for learning and self-reflection, propelling me further along the path of personal development.

As I immersed myself in this journey of self-discovery, I discovered the profound joy and fulfillment that comes from expanding my knowledge, honing my skills, and cultivating new talents. Each new challenge I encountered served as a catalyst for growth, pushing me to stretch beyond my perceived limitations and unlock hidden reservoirs of potential.

Moreover, I came to understand that success is not a solitary pursuit but a collaborative endeavor. I sought out mentors, coaches, and like-minded individuals who could inspire, support, and guide me along the way. Their wisdom, encouragement, and invaluable insights enriched my journey and accelerated my progress towards my goals.

Through this commitment to self-development and growth, I embraced the journey of becoming the best version of myself. I recognized that true success is not measured solely by external achievements but by the depth of character, resilience, and wisdom gained along the way. It is a journey of lifelong learning and evolution, fueled by an insatiable curiosity and a relentless drive to become the greatest expression of myself.

Getting Into the Practice of Being a Lifelong Learner

As I arrived at a pivotal juncture in my journey, I came to a profound realization: personal growth is not a finite destination but an ongoing process of evolution and self-discovery. Initially, I may have harbored the notion that there would come a point where I would have "arrived" at some ultimate state of mastery or enlightenment. However, I soon understood that true growth requires an unwavering commitment to lifelong learning and self-improvement.

With this newfound perspective, I embraced the idea that investing in oneself is not a one-time endeavor but a lifelong journey. I recognized that there would always be more to learn, explore, and discover. This realization fueled my determination to continually seek out opportunities for growth and development, knowing that knowledge is a powerful tool that empowers us to navigate life's challenges and seize opportunities.

To this end, I pursued various avenues of learning, ranging from formal education to informal self-study. I enrolled in courses relevant to my field of work, eager to deepen my expertise and stay abreast of the latest developments in my industry. Additionally, I devoted time to reading books on personal development, leadership, and mindfulness, recognizing the invaluable insights they offered for both my professional and personal growth.

Each new piece of knowledge I acquired became a building block in my journey of self-improvement, contributing to my growth as an individual and a professional. Whether through formal education, reading, attending workshops, or seeking mentorship, I remained steadfast in my commitment to expanding my knowledge and honing my skills.

In doing so, I embraced the philosophy that learning is a lifelong endeavor, and that every experience, encounter, and lesson has the potential to enrich our lives and deepen our understanding of the world around us. By remaining open to new ideas and experiences, I continue to evolve and grow, knowing that the journey of self-discovery is one that unfolds endlessly, offering limitless opportunities for growth and transformation.

Pawsitivity Unleashed

Learning to Step Out of the Comfort Zone

In the journey of personal growth, I discovered that many of the most significant leaps forward occurred when I ventured beyond the confines of my comfort zone. Stepping into unfamiliar territory and embracing discomfort became a deliberate strategy for catalyzing growth and transformation. I recognized that true growth often requires us to confront our fears, push past self-imposed limitations, and explore uncharted territory.

With this understanding, I made a conscious effort to seek out new experiences that challenged me and expanded my horizons. This could manifest in various forms, from taking on daunting projects at work to embarking on solo adventures to unfamiliar destinations. Each instance provided an opportunity to test my boundaries, stretch my capabilities, and discover untapped reservoirs of resilience and courage within myself.

One particularly memorable experience that exemplifies this principle was my decision to explore the concept of hypnotism. It was a field that had always intrigued me, yet I had never ventured into it before. Undeterred by my lack of experience, I committed myself wholeheartedly to the pursuit, enrolling in classes and dedicating time each day to practice and study.

The journey into hypnotism was not without its challenges. There were moments of frustration and self-doubt, times when progress seemed elusive. However, I refused to be deterred, drawing upon my inner reserves of perseverance and determination to push forward.

Through dedication and persistence, I gradually began to unravel the complexities of hypnotism, honing my skills and deepening my understanding of the subject. The process was both humbling and empowering, serving as a testament to the transformative power of resilience and grit.

In the end, my efforts bore fruit, culminating in a sense of achievement and mastery that reaffirmed my belief in the boundless potential of the human spirit. The experience taught me invaluable lessons about the importance of embracing discomfort, persisting in the face of adversity, and trusting in the process of growth and self-discovery.

Learning to Cope & Find Resilience When Faced with Challenges

One of the most profound realizations on my journey toward success was the acceptance of imperfection as an inherent part of the human experience. I came to understand that failures are not definitive endpoints but rather opportunities for growth and learning. Embracing this mindset shift allowed me to view challenges not as insurmountable obstacles but as steppingstones on the path to personal and professional development.

In the past, I had held onto limiting beliefs that equated failure with inadequacy, leading to a cycle of frustration and self-doubt. However, through introspection and self-awareness, I began to recognize the fallacy of these beliefs. I came to understand that true strength lies not in avoiding failure but in how we respond to it—with resilience, determination, and a willingness to learn.

Each setback I encountered became an opportunity to test and strengthen my resilience. Whether facing professional setbacks or personal hardships, I approached each challenge with a newfound sense of resilience and determination. Instead of allowing setbacks to derail me, I used them as fuel to propel me forward, refusing to let adversity define my path.

Pawsitivity Unleashed

By cultivating resilience, I learned to navigate life's inevitable difficulties with grace and perseverance. I discovered that setbacks are not reflections of my worth or abilities but simply part of the journey toward success. With each obstacle overcome, I emerged stronger, more resilient, and better equipped to face whatever challenges lay ahead.

Resilience became my guiding light, illuminating the path forward and reminding me of my inherent strength and resilience in the face of adversity. Through embracing imperfection and harnessing the power of resilience, I have learned to approach life's challenges with courage, grace, and unwavering determination.

Using Failure as a Steppingstone

Failure, far from being a roadblock, has become an integral part of my journey toward success. It serves as a valuable teacher, offering insights and lessons that propel me forward on my path. Rather than viewing failure as a sign of inadequacy or defeat, I have learned to embrace it as a necessary step in the process of growth and development.

One of the most transformative experiences occurred when a project I had invested significant time and effort into failed to meet expectations. Initially, I felt disheartened and discouraged by the outcome. However, instead of allowing myself to be consumed by defeat, I chose to approach the situation with a growth mindset.

I took the time to reflect on the factors that contributed to the project's shortcomings, conducting a thorough analysis of what went wrong. This process of introspection allowed me to identify specific areas for improvement and areas where I could refine my approach in the future.

Armed with this newfound insight, I made a conscious effort to apply the lessons learned from my failure. When a similar opportunity presented itself, I approached it with renewed determination and a clear plan of action. Drawing upon the wisdom gained from my previous experience, I navigated the challenges with confidence and resilience.

The result was a significant improvement in the outcome of the project, demonstrating the transformative power of failure when approached with the right mindset. Rather than allowing failure to derail me, I used it as a catalyst for growth and improvement. In doing so, I discovered that failure is not the end of the road but rather a steppingstone on the path to success.

Practicing Resilience in the Face of Adversity

During moments of personal adversity, such as grappling with the loss of a loved one or confronting health challenges, I found solace in my resilience, which became my guiding light through the darkest of times. Through these trials, I came to understand the paramount importance of self-care, the value of seeking support from cherished ones, and the practice of mindfulness to safeguard my mental and emotional well-being.

One of the most formidable challenges I encountered was when I confronted unexpected financial hardships. This period plunged me into a whirlwind of stress and uncertainty, threatening to overwhelm me. However, I refused to succumb to despair. Instead, I made a conscious decision to confront the situation head-on.

Armed with determination and a newfound sense of resolve, I devised a comprehensive plan to address my financial woes. I sought guidance from trusted financial advisors, who provided invaluable insights and support every step of the way. Together, we charted a course of action designed to navigate the complexities of my financial predicament.

The journey toward financial stability was neither swift nor effortless. It demanded unwavering commitment, perseverance, and resilience in the face of adversity. There were moments of doubt and discouragement, but I refused to be deterred. With each obstacle encountered, I leaned into my resilience, drawing strength from within to press onward.

Through sheer determination and perseverance, I gradually began to see progress. Small victories served as beacons of hope amidst the darkness, fueling my resolve to keep pushing forward. Despite the challenges and setbacks along the way, I remained steadfast in my pursuit of financial stability.

My resilience proved to be my greatest asset. It carried me through the toughest of times, instilling in me a sense of resilience and fortitude that I never knew I possessed. As I emerged from the depths of adversity, I did so with a renewed sense of strength and resilience, ready to face whatever challenges lay ahead.

Taking A Holistic Approach to Success

My journey toward success has been a dynamic and intricate one, shaped by the fundamental principles of mindset, self-development, and resilience. These guiding principles have propelled me forward, fostering personal and professional growth in profound ways.

Embracing a growth mindset has been paramount in my journey. By cultivating a mindset focused on continuous learning and improvement, I have opened myself up to endless possibilities for growth and development. This mindset has enabled me to approach challenges with optimism and determination, viewing them not as roadblocks but as opportunities for learning and growth.

Committing to continuous self-improvement has been another cornerstone of my journey. I have dedicated myself to ongoing learning and development, seeking out new knowledge and skills to expand my horizons. Whether through formal education, self-directed study, or experiential learning, I have embraced every opportunity to enhance my capabilities and deepen my understanding of the world around me.

Most importantly, resilience has been my steadfast companion throughout my journey. In the face of adversity and setbacks, I have drawn upon my inner strength and determination to persevere. I have learned to navigate challenges with grace and resilience, refusing to be deterred by temporary setbacks or obstacles.

Success, I have come to realize, is not a destination but a journey of self-discovery and growth. It is about the person I become along the way—the lessons I learn, the obstacles I overcome, and the growth I achieve. As I reflect on my journey thus far, I am filled with gratitude for the experiences that have shaped me and the opportunities that lie ahead.

Looking to the future, I am excited for the road ahead. With the right mindset, dedication to self-improvement, and resilience, I am confident that I can continue to achieve success in all areas of my life. Each day presents new opportunities for growth and discovery, and I am committed to embracing them wholeheartedly.

Learning to Draw Valuable Parallels

In the journey of self-discovery and personal growth, we begin a quest for inspiration and guidance, exploring various sources for wisdom and insight. Remarkably, one often overlooks the wellspring of profound wisdom lies within the principles of foundational dog training. While this connection may initially seem unexpected, the parallels between training our beloved canine companions and nurturing our own personal foundation are nothing short of extraordinary. As we look deeper into these parallels, we will unveil the ways in which the fundamental principles of dog training can serve as invaluable guides on your journey of self-discovery, just as they have for me. By embracing these parallels, you can unlock profound insights and accelerate your progress on the path to personal development, saving yourself countless hours of searching for answers and navigating the complexities of your inner journey.

What is the Significance of Building Strong Foundations

Before looking into the parallels between dog training principles and personal development, it's essential to underscore the significance of building a robust foundation. Just as a sturdy foundation is indispensable for erecting a stable building, a strong personal foundation serves as the bedrock of your life's structure. This foundation encompasses your values, beliefs, habits, and mindset – the fundamental elements that define your identity and govern your decisions and actions.

Likewise, with dog training, establishing a solid foundation is paramount to successfully training a new canine companion. Whether you're imparting basic obedience commands or addressing behavioral issues, laying the groundwork with clear communication, consistency, and patience lays the groundwork for effective training and facilitates long-term behavior modification. By recognizing the importance of building a strong foundation in both personal development and dog training, we can appreciate the parallels between these disparate domains and leverage them to accelerate our growth and progress.

What Parallels Can Be Found in Clarity and Communication?

One of the striking parallels between foundational dog training and a personal foundation lies in clarity and communication. In dog training, clear communication between the trainer and their dog is essential for conveying expectations and reinforcing desired behaviors. Likewise, when you are working on your own personal development journey, clarity in your purpose and having effective self-communication are vital for you to be able to align your actions with goals and values.

For instance, when a dog trainer communicates commands through verbal cues and body language, you must communicate your intentions and aspirations with clarity and conviction. By defining values, setting clear goals, and establishing boundaries, you create a roadmap for your own personal growth and fulfillment.

The Parallels Can Be Found in Consistency and Discipline?

Another parallel between dog training and personal development is in the principles of consistency and discipline. In dog training, consistency reinforces desired behaviors and builds trust between a trainer and their dog. Similarly, in personal development, consistency in habits and routines is essential for achieving goals and fostering self-discipline.

For example, just as a dog trainer sets a consistent training schedule and follows through with reinforcement, you must commit to daily practices that support their own growth and well-being. Whether it is regular exercise, mindfulness, or pursuing learning opportunities, consistency leads to progress and cultivates resilience.

The Parallels Can Be Found in Adaptability and Resilience?

Both dog training and personal development require adaptability and resilience in navigating obstacles and setbacks. In dog training, trainers adjust their approach based on each dog's needs, remaining patient and adaptable. Likewise, you must embrace change and setbacks as opportunities for growth, allowing you to remain resilient in adversity.

For instance, just as a dog trainer modifies techniques to address behavioral challenges, you must adapt strategies and mindset to overcome obstacles. By cultivating resilience and learning from your setbacks, you begin to strengthen your own personal foundation and become adept at facing life's uncertainties.

The Parallels Can Be Found in Building Trust and Connection?

Finally, both dog training and personal development also emphasize the importance of building trust and connection in relationships. In dog training, trust between a trainer and dog is the foundation of effective communication and a strong bond. Similarly, in a journey to personal development, trust in oneself and others fosters meaningful connections and supports growth.

For example, just as a dog trainer builds trust through consistent reinforcement, you build trust with yourself through self-compassion and honoring your values. By nurturing trusting relationships with others, you begin to create a supportive network for personal growth and resilience.

The parallels between the foundations of dog training and personal foundations highlight the interconnectedness of both different domains. By drawing upon the principles of clarity, communication, consistency, adaptability, and trust, you can enrich your journey of self-discovery and personal development.

Whether training a dog in obedience or navigating your own personal growth, the principles remain will remain the same; clarity of purpose, consistent effort, adaptability, and trust are essential for success. By recognizing and embracing these parallels, you can leverage the lessons learned from life or dog training to build a strong personal foundation, creating a life filled with purpose, resilience, and joy.

8

Chapter Eight

My Reinvention & Rediscovery

Out with the Old & Embracing the New You

My journey of reinvention has been a thrilling yet challenging one. Rediscovering my true self, embracing authenticity, and accepting all the aspects of myself I once judged harshly has been incredibly rewarding. It is all too easy to accumulate negative thoughts and comments, carrying them like bricks in a backpack that weigh on the mind and body until change becomes necessary, or we risk being buried beneath their weight.

I used to think that once you have reinvented yourself and know who you are and what you want, the process becomes easier. In some ways, it does. However, with this newfound clarity comes higher expectations for oneself and those around you. This can pose its own set of challenges, especially when others have not done the same inner work. But that is all right. Do not be disheartened. It is all part of growing into your new self. Throughout this journey, I have learned patience, empathy, acceptance, respect, and kindness. I have realized that even if I considered myself the kindest person, there was always room for improvement. It is a journey of constant change.

Some days were exhilarating. My mind felt clear, the air seemed fresher, my body lighter, and I was charged with excitement to achieve more. Other days, I felt utterly exhausted. I struggled to keep up with myself, grappling with thoughts and ideas I had held onto for decades. I was rediscovering myself while shedding the negative energy that had long plagued me with frustration and impatience.

The biggest hurdle in my reinvention was learning to sit in silence. To just be. To be okay with not being productive, active, or constantly busy. I had filled my life with activities to avoid confronting underlying issues. But this silence was not meditation, although I sometimes meditated during it. For someone like me, always needing to be busy, always needing to feel productive, sitting quietly was a monumental challenge.

Here is where Heidi, my loyal companion, played a crucial role in my journey. She comforted me in those quiet moments, lying by my side, my constant companion. She was my "ride or die" friend who never left me. When I had to confront my thoughts and feelings in those moments of silence, she was there, a grounding presence. This process brought forth a flood of emotions. It forced me to confront unresolved feelings from my childhood, the grief of an abusive relationship with my son's father, the struggles of being a single mother, and the adjustments to my new roles as a military spouse and mother of a blended family of four.

Sitting in the quiet with Heidi seemed to peel away layers of darkness, allowing my true self to shine through. It was not an easy journey, and there were days of discomfort. I had to learn to be comfortable with being uncomfortable, knowing that this discomfort signaled growth and change. Little by little, the weight of the bricks in my metaphorical backpack lightened.

Looking back after two weeks, a month, three months, I could see the changes. I smiled and laughed more than I was sad or down. Things that used to bother me no longer held power. I started enjoying activities I used to love, exploring new hobbies, and wanting to take better care of myself. The ripple effect was in motion. I noticed I was losing weight, and the people around me seemed happier too. My reinvention was not just changing me; it was positively impacting those around me.

I owe a great deal of gratitude to Heidi, as these challenging moments were the most transformative. Once I became consistent

Pawsitivity Unleashed

with this process, it became my new normal. Living in the quiet, seeking refuge and meditation in it, has become my way of staying grounded and confident. I would never go back to the old way of avoiding stillness and introspection. This quiet, this reinvention, has become my only way to truly live.

In my own experience, and through the experience of others, here are the key lessons learned to guarantee a successful reinvention for yourself.

Lessons for A Successful Reinvention Journey

Embracing Reinvention

Life, much like dog training, requires a willingness to reinvent us. When a dog comes to me with behavioral issues, I do not see a lost cause; I see potential. The same goes for our own lives. We must approach challenges with an open mind and a belief that change is possible.

Lesson 1: Embrace Change

Just as I adapt my training methods to suit each dog's needs, we must adapt to life's changes. Sometimes, what once worked no longer does, and that is okay. Embracing change means letting go of the fear of the unknown and trusting in our ability to learn and grow.

Pawsitivity Unleashed

Lesson 2: Persistence Pays Off

Reinvention takes time and patience. When teaching a new behavior to a dog, it is not achieved in a single session. It requires consistent effort and repetition. Similarly, in life, progress may be gradual, but each step forward is a victory.

Overcoming Obstacles

In both dog training and life, obstacles are inevitable. Whether it is a stubborn behavior or a personal setback, how we approach these challenges determines our success.

Lesson 3: Break it Down.

When faced with a complex behavior problem in a dog, I break it down into smaller, manageable steps. This approach prevents overwhelm and allows for steady progress. In life, daunting goals become achievable when we break them into smaller tasks.

Lesson 4: Patience and understanding

Not every dog responds immediately, and the same goes for us. Patience and understanding, both for the dog and for us, are key. It is about acknowledging that setbacks happen and using them as learning opportunities.

Pawsitivity Unleashed

Discovering Purpose and Passion

Dogs have an uncanny ability to live in the present moment and find joy in the simplest of things. We can learn a lot from their zest for life when it comes to finding our own purpose and passion.

Lesson 5: Follow Your Tail

Dogs do not worry about what others think; they follow their instincts. Similarly, finding purpose means tapping into what genuinely excites and fulfills us, regardless of external expectations. Whether it is a career change or a new hobby, listen to your inner voice.

Lesson 6: Celebrate Small Wins

In dog training, we celebrate every small success along the way. It keeps motivation high and builds momentum. In life, acknowledging and celebrating our achievements, no matter how small, fuels our drive towards bigger goals.

Pawsitive Principles for Life

The principles I have learned from dog training are not just about obedience; they are life skills that can guide us towards a more fulfilling and purpose-driven life.

Principle 1: Positive Reinforcement

Using treats and praise to reinforce good behavior in dogs is a powerful tool. In life, positive reinforcement means focusing on what we are doing right rather than dwelling on mistakes. It is about cultivating a mindset of growth and progress.

Principle 2: Clear Communication

Dogs respond best to clear, consistent cues. Likewise, effective communication in life, whether with others or with us, is crucial. Clearly define your goals and intentions and communicate them assertively.

Principle 3: Adaptability

Every dog is unique, requiring different approaches. Similarly, life throws curveballs that require us to adapt and be flexible. Being rigid leads to frustration, while adaptability opens doors to new opportunities.

Pawsitivity Unleashed

Principle 4: Trust and Connection

The bond between a dog and its trainer is built on trust. In life, trusting ourselves and cultivating meaningful connections with others are pillars of a fulfilling existence. Surround yourself with those who uplift and support your journey.

In the journey of life, we are both the trainer and the student. By applying the principles of dog training to our own lives, we can overcome obstacles, discover our purpose, and embrace reinvention. Remember, it is not about perfection but progress. Celebrate each step forward, no matter how small, and trust in your ability to unleash your full potential. As you navigate this journey, remember the pawsitive lessons from our four-legged friends – they hold the keys to a purposeful and passionate life.

Reflecting on Your Reinvention and Next Steps

Congratulations on Your Incredible Progress. If you have been diligently working through your workbook and journaling, I am extremely proud of you. By now, you should have gained new insights into your own story, its impact on you, and you have already outlined your plan for the changes and goals you have for yourself in the upcoming weeks.

Pawsitivity Unleashed

I want to commend you for the incredible journey you have started. Your dedication and hard work in laying the foundation, promoting positivity, and embracing change are truly admirable. Your commitment to personal growth and improvement is commendable, and I applaud every step you have taken on this transformative path so far.

Approaching Reinvention with Enthusiasm

As you begin to focus on the next stage of your journey, which can be the most transcendental, I ask you to move forward with an open mind, open heart, and enthusiasm. This is an exciting time. Your reinvention! A chance to do it all over again. I encourage you to approach it with the same enthusiasm and determination that has brought you this far. When we talk about embracing the concept of reinvention—a concept that may seem daunting initially however, it holds immense promise and potential for both personal and professional growth.

Continuing to reflect on your own journey, I want to remind you that reinvention is not merely about making small tweaks; it is about daring to dream big, taking big risks and embracing new opportunities and possibilities. Just as I transformed my passion for animals into a successful career and business, you too have the power to do the same. Take the time to dream and reimagine your life the way you have always wanted it. Pursue the passions you long avoided because you thought they would not offer much for a career. Meditate and dig deeper than you have ever done before. This is YOUR time, your chance to do and be anything you ever wanted. If you are still unsure, take the time to discover the hobbies you always had an interest in until the answer comes to you. I promise the answer will come to you and remember do it all with purpose and enthusiasm.

Signs of Progress During Reinvention

I often get questions at this stage, which include "How do I know if I am making any progress?" or "After all this work, is it working? I do not feel any different." In both self-transformation and dog training, there are several signs of progress that can serve as indicators of growth and development.

Achieving Clarity and Direction

When someone finds clarity, or direction in their story, their journey, these are signs of progress. You may find this newfound sense of clarity and direction emerges as you engage in creative exercises and brainstorming sessions. It can also lead you to clarity or a better understanding of your goals, values, and aspirations, guiding you towards a more fulfilling and purpose-driven life.

Pawsitivity Unleashed

Noticing Improved Communication

Progress often manifests itself in improved communication and understanding between you and your furry companion. As you begin to implement new training techniques, you may notice subtle shifts in your dog's behavior and responsiveness, indicating progress made together. Similarly, it can also be seen in your communication with others and yourself on your own personal journey. Your abilities and skills sharpen as you invest in yourself and your journey and in that process your communication skills become more effective.

Willingness to Embrace Change

Progress in reinvention often involves stepping out of your comfort zone and embracing change. Just as I took bold risks to pursue my dreams, you will begin to find yourself exploring new avenues and taking calculated risks in pursuit of your goals as well. You will be more likely to embrace change, and less fearful of it. You may even find you become more confident in your abilities to handle these changes with the skills you learn through your thirty-day journey.

Empowerment and Confidence

Overcoming obstacles and achieving milestones can lead to a sense of empowerment and confidence. This newfound confidence serves as fuel to propel you forward, inspiring you to continue pushing boundaries.

Lessons from Dog Training

In the realm of dog training, progress is accompanied by a willingness to adapt and evolve your approach. Flexibility and open-mindedness are key as you navigate the ever-changing landscape of canine behavior and training.

Just as progress in reinvention breeds confidence, both in yourself and in your dog, witnessing the positive impact of your efforts can boost confidence in your ability to shape behavior and foster a strong bond based on trust and mutual respect.

Embracing Your Journey

The journey of reinvention is ongoing, requiring patience, perseverance, and a willingness to embrace change. Drawing inspiration from my story and applying the principles of creativity, courage, and determination to your life can unlock your full potential.

As you continue your journey, take a moment to reflect on the signs of progress you have already made. Celebrate how far you have come and remember that reinvention is about embracing the entire process, with all its growth and transformation.

Seize these little moments and opportunities to daydream and reimagine your life. Explore new possibilities and do not be afraid to dream bigger than you ever did before. Do not cap your goals. Do not limit your abilities. When you hear negative thoughts, actively push them away and say something positive in their place. Remember, if you have not tried it, you do not know if you are good at it or if you would even like or enjoy it. Be open-minded to new possibilities, try new things, new hobbies, new projects. The only limits we have are the limits we put on ourselves.

The Transformative Power of SMART Goals

As I reflect on my journey to reinvention, one tool that has been instrumental in guiding me was the concept of SMART goals Let me share with you how this framework transformed my approach to goal setting and helped me navigate through the process of reinventing myself.

Imagine finding yourself at a crossroads, overwhelmed by the changes you want to make. You know you need a clear roadmap but are not sure where to start. This happened to me many times before my transformative journey. There are even times I still refer to SMART goals today. These skills we learn and discuss are not just skills for thirty days these are applicable life skills you use regularly, sometime daily. Successful people use this skill all the time. They manage and structure their day and utilize the skills we review in this thirty-day plan on a regular basis to keep their mind sharp and well oiled.

You are your biggest investment. We get tired, worn out, overwhelmed and depressed because we stop doing all the things within these exercises you are doing over the next thirty days. It is so easy to complete the workbook, journal and after thirty days, slip right back into your old habits and that is when you find the same thoughts and feelings, dissatisfaction kick right back in. Life happens and family needs you, the kids need you, work needs you and then you find yourself at the bottom of the list with all you need being last on the list. That is half the reason we get this feeling of being unfulfilled, lost, and overwhelmed. The only way to change that is to make small doable changes over thirty days that will create new healthy routines that you can maintain that support you and a healthy mind, space, thought and attitude. That is your new foundation. You do that with the skills or exercises we work on over the next thirty days and the changes will just come. From there you can begin to create the life you have always wanted. One that also includes being surrounded by supportive people who cheer you on in whatever you do. You begin to integrate what you love into your life, activities, hobbies, even a new career! You utilize what you learn about SMART goals to help you build on that. Remember, I was once where you are right now. I knew about SMART goals before I started working with them, however I was not using them correctly. I almost dismissed the journey for lack of knowledge or for lack of a better word, too much knowledge. Sometimes we have done so much work that going back to the beginning seems mundane and irrelevant. I am here to tell you it is not. But Heck, there were a few times in my life I did think I knew better and thought going through the motions was pointless, yet I was never able to find an alternative solution and I always circled back to the fundamentals I am providing you today. It is because they seem so simple, yet we have not mastered them. We need to practice and continue to invest in the work. It is ongoing. If you take the time over the next 30 days to put in the work to do the exercises you will see the results. I even give you supplementary exercises for all four weeks either for additional work for the first four weeks or an additional thirty days! So, what is this simple yet powerful framework you ask? Well, let us talk about it.

What are SMART Goals & Why are they so Significant?

SMART stands for Specific, Measurable, Achievable, Relevant, and Time-bound. This framework, introduced by George T. Doran, provides a structured approach to setting objectives giving each letter a meaning:

Pawsitivity Unleashed

- **Specific:** Clearly defined goals leave no room for ambiguity. For example, "I will lose 10 pounds in 10 weeks."
- **Measurable:** Goals should include criteria for measuring progress. "I will exercise for 30 minutes five days a week."
- **Achievable:** Ensure goals are realistic given your circumstances. "I will follow a balanced diet."
- **Relevant:** Goals should align with your objectives. "I want to lead a healthier lifestyle."
- **Time-bound:** A defined timeline creates urgency. "I will achieve this in 10 weeks."

How Do You Transform Your Vague Desires into Tangible Objectives?

When you apply the SMART criteria to your goal setting, abstract desires become concrete action plans. Regularly reviewing and adjusting these goals keeps you on track. *Here is an example comparison of a SMART goal versus a non-SMART goal.*

This is an example of what a Non-SMART Goal looks like:

"I want to get in shape."

The statement lacks specificity, measurability, achievability, relevance, and a time limit. You need more detail! It is over generalization that makes it too fluid and not concrete making the action less likely for you to successfully complete the task. You just do not know how too.

Pawsitivity Unleashed

This is an example of what a quality SMART goal looks like:

"I will lose 10 pounds in the next 10 weeks by exercising for at least 30 minutes five days a week and following a balanced diet. I will track my progress weekly."

This SMART goal provides a clear roadmap for success! It meets all the five objectives. It is specific, measurable, achievable, relevant and has a time limit or goal.

Why Should I Embrace the Power of SMART Goals?

SMART goals have been around and used by organizations and different industries for years because of their successful results. SMART goals are invaluable tools and you have come across them once or twice before. You will find companies reference them in their training programs, coaching classes, leadership development programs, even military training classes. So, when you find yourself on a journey of reinvention, and you are looking to create or set clear actionable goals with objectives this would be the system to use. As you become better at making your goals meet all the criteria, and practicing until it becomes second nature will help you with that, once it becomes second nature you will see how the SMART goals become your outline to success for your goal and you are then able to navigate with confidence.

Pawsitivity Unleashed

One of my favorites saying when it comes to SMART goals is that "The devil is in the details" which means that the small, often overlooked elements of a plan or situation can cause major problems later. So, it is suggested that you pay careful attention to even the smallest details to avoid complications or failures. Long ago, I was one to rush through things, I did not have the patience as I do now. This is going back to my youth. I do not think many of us can say we are as patient now as we were twenty-five years ago. However, when I rushed through things I missed the details. The details were vital. Now sometimes I get away with it, but when I got older, college exams got harder, work expectations grew, it was in the details that set you apart from the crowd. In many industries, knowing the details was a necessity to success. When I went into Finance, the details were crucial. I had to slow down and take in the details. It made the difference in the production of work, the meeting of goals and more. So, take your time, and focus on the details of each of your goals.

The small details you create and add to make an effective SMART goal are the necessary pieces you need to ensure that you are successful in meeting your own goals. It gives you better guidelines and path to follow. When it is over generalized like a non-SMART goal, you are more likely to lead an ineffective meeting or not meet that personal goal.

In a recent study on effects of a SMART goal setting, a twelve-week core strength training intervention on Physical fitness and Exercise Attitudes for Adolescents conducted a randomized controlled Trial done by Yijuan Lu Kehong Yu and Xiaomei Gan to see if there were benefits of using SMART GOALS. They uncovered those adolescents that participated in the core strength training class were more effective when it was combined with using the SMART goal techniques (Lu, Yu, & Gan, 2022).

The students that did not participate in the SMART goal techniques showed little to minimal lack of interest and or improvement in physical fitness. It was only when the students combined the smart goals with the fitness program, did the trial see any benefit. This is just one study. There have been many other studies done on whether SMART goals bring value to the individual and the benefits are all seen when SMART goals are utilized.

I know that once I added SMART goals into my vocabulary and started setting goals based off the criteria, I saw an instant increase in productivity. I found it easier and clearer to meet my goal. Over generalization allowed for error, room for too much change, acceptance for not exactly meeting the goal and thus ineffective leaders, people and more. With a SMART goal there was no ambiguity on how to meet the goal. It created a more productive team, and easier ways for leaders and managers to recognize their team when they meet their goals. The benefits outweighed not using them.

Pawsitivity Unleashed

Reinforcing the New Me with My Furry Companion

Embarking on a journey of rediscovery and reinvention is a profound and transformative experience. Celebrating successes and milestones along this path becomes crucial in reinforcing the new positive habits and behaviors you are looking to create. Through training, my own journey, and my standard poodle Heidi I have strengthened our bond and cherished every achievement along the way.

The Power of Positive Reinforcement

In dog training, positive reinforcement is a fundamental and potent tool for shaping behaviors and fostering a strong bond between the trainer and the dog. Instead of focusing on punishment or correction, positive reinforcement involves rewarding the desired behaviors to encourage the dog's repetition. This approach not only teaches new skills but also builds trust and enhances relationships between the dog and human handler.

Similarly, in the journey of self-discovery or when you are working on your own reinvention, celebrating successes also plays a vital role in reinforcing your own positive habits and behaviors. By acknowledging and rewarding your progress, you become more motivated to continue forward on your path of personal growth. Whether it is achieving a fitness goal, mastering a new skill, or overcoming a challenge, each milestone is a cause for celebration and a reminder of your resilience.

Strengthening the Bond with Heidi

Heidi has been my faithful companion; she has been by my side through every step of my journey. Through dog training exercises and daily interactions, we have deepened our connection and strengthened our bond. Each successful training session is not just a testament to Heidi's intelligence but also a reflection of our strong partnership and mutual trust.

Just as I celebrate Heidi's achievements in mastering new commands or behaviors, she celebrates my successes in overcoming obstacles too. Our bond grows stronger with each shared victory, reinforcing our commitment to supporting each other through life's challenges.

My Ongoing Journey to Reclaim My New Self

In my personal journey, as I navigated through the stages of rediscovery, reinvention, and reclaiming myself, Heidi remained a steadfast companion. She was the unwavering rock amidst the tumultuous battles I faced, and she joyfully embraced the new adventures and experiences we shared together. Each day became an opportunity for growth and self-reflection, and we celebrated every

Pawsitivity Unleashed

success, no matter how small, as a reminder of both my progress and her development in training. We were a team, embarking on this journey together.

By incorporating daily exercises and engaging in creative exploratory activities, we ventured into new passions and challenges together. Whether it was experimenting with a new hobby, pursuing a cherished dream, or simply basking in the beauty of a park or embarking on a road trip, each day became a celebration of our authentic selves.

Celebrating Success

Celebrating milestones and successes became second nature, and it was hugely enjoyable. Heidi relished the extra treats, car rides, and toys, while I cherished her companionship. These celebrations became an integral part of my journey to rediscover, reinvent, and reclaim myself. Whether it was training Heidi or focusing on my personal growth, positive reinforcement became a powerful tool that strengthened my determination and deepened my connection not only with Heidi but also with those around me.

With Heidi faithfully by my side, every achievement became a celebration of our resilience and unbreakable bond. Together, we forge ahead on our journey, embracing each day's opportunities for growth and change.

Pawsitivity Unleashed

9

Chapter Nine

My Path to Unleashing Potential

Embracing Change, Finding Purpose, & Igniting Passion

In life, there comes a time when we feel a stirring within us, a yearning for something more. This was the point at which I found myself not too long ago, standing at a crossroads of uncertainty and possibility. It was a moment of introspection, where I realized that I wanted to unleash my potential, to embrace change, and to rediscover my purpose and passion. Little did I know that this journey would not only reshape my mindset but also lead me down a path of self-development, growth, resilience, and coping.

The first step on this transformative journey was to shift my mindset. I realized that my thoughts and beliefs about myself and the world around me influenced my actions and outcomes. I decided to adopt a growth mindset, a belief that my abilities and intelligence could be developed through dedication and hard work. This mindset approach allowed me to see challenges as opportunities for growth rather than obstacles.

To facilitate this mindset shift, I turned to resources like journaling. Journaling became my sanctuary, a safe space where I could pour out my thoughts, fears, and aspirations. It allowed me to gain clarity, reflect on my progress, and set intentions for the future. Creating a roadmap was another crucial step. I defined my goals with precision, breaking them down into actionable steps. This roadmap was not just a list of dreams; it was a concrete plan that guided me forward.

Breaking down my goals into smaller, achievable steps was a significant change. It made the insurmountable tasks feel manageable. Each small victory fueled my motivation and propelled me further along the path of self-discovery. I learned the power of positive reinforcement, celebrating even the smallest wins along the way. This positivity infused my journey with joy and excitement.

However, embracing change and unleashing potential is not always a smooth ride. Challenges inevitably arise, and this is where resilience and coping strategies come into play. I learned that setbacks were not failures but opportunities to learn and grow. When faced with obstacles, I practiced resilience by bouncing back stronger than before.

Consistency became my mantra. I understood that true growth and change require persistent effort over time. I learned to trust the process, even when progress seemed slow. Patience became my ally, reminding me that transformation is a journey, not a sprint. I persisted, day after day, trusting that each step forward was bringing me closer to my goals.

One of the most significant lessons I learned on this journey was the art of pivoting. Life is unpredictable and plans often need to be adjusted. Instead of being rigid in my approach, I learned to pivot gracefully when circumstances changed. This flexibility allowed me to adapt and grow in unexpected ways.

Through it all, I discovered the resilience within me. I faced moments of doubt and fear, but I refused to let them define me. Instead, I leaned into discomfort, knowing that growth often lies just beyond our comfort zones. I developed coping strategies to navigate the rough patches, whether it was meditation, exercise, or seeking support from loved ones.

Pawsitivity Unleashed

As I reflect on this journey, I realize that it was not just about achieving external success but about the internal transformation that took place. I reignited my passion by reconnecting with what truly mattered to me. I found purpose in aligning my actions with my values and beliefs. I reinvented myself by shedding old limiting beliefs and embracing a new, empowered identity.

Today, I stand before you as a testament to the power of mind-set, self-development, growth, resilience, and coping. This journey has been a rollercoaster of emotions, but every twist and turn has been worth it. I have emerged stronger, wiser, and more aligned with my true self.

To anyone embarking on a similar journey, I offer these words of encouragement: embrace change, define your goals, take con-sistent action, celebrate your wins, trust the process, pivot when needed, cultivate resilience, and remember to be kind to yourself along the way. Your potential is limitless, waiting to be unleashed. It is not about reaching the destination; it is about the growth and transformation that occur along the way. So, dare to dream big, and embark on the journey of a lifetime.

Taking the Next Steps to Unleash Your Full Potential Embracing Changes Ahead

Change can be daunting, especially when it comes to finding our purpose reigniting passion or reinventing yourself. But just like training a dog, it is all about taking small steps, being patient, and embracing the process.

Step 1: Define Your Destination

When I train a dog, I always start with a clear goal in mind. Similarly, in life, it is crucial to define what you want to achieve. Take some time to reflect on your own passions, values, and what truly makes you come alive. Write down your goals, both short-term and long-term. This clarity will serve as your compass, guiding you towards your purpose.

Step 2: Break It Down into Achievable Steps

Training a dog to perform a complex trick requires breaking it down into manageable steps. The same principle applies to your own goals. Divide your journey into smaller, achievable milestones. This not only makes the path less overwhelming, but it also gives you a sense of accomplishment as you can begin to check off each step.

Pawsitivity Unleashed

Step 3: Embrace the Learning Process

Dogs do not learn tricks overnight, and neither do we as humans, master a new skill instantly. So, embrace the learning process with an open mind and a willingness to make mistakes. Every stumble is a lesson in disguise, leading you closer to your potential. Remember, it is not about perfection; it is about progress.

Step 4: Adapt and Pivot

In dog training, flexibility is so important. If a certain method is not working, I need to recognize it and adjust my approach. Similarly, in life, I also need to be willing to adapt and pivot when it is needed. Unexpected challenges arise all the time, but they are opportunities for growth. Do not be afraid to try new paths or explore different passions along the way. It can open new doors you had not thought of or expected.

Applying Pawsitive Principles to Unleash Your Potential

Now, let us dive into the pawsitive principles that have transformed not just the behavior of dogs but also the lives of many people just like yourself. These principles are not just for training dogs; they are also great for training ourselves on how to lead a fulfilling life.

Pawsitivity Unleashed

Principle 1: Positive Reinforcement

In dog training, positive reinforcement involves rewarding desired behaviors. In life, this principle translates to acknowledging and celebrating your progress. When you achieve a milestone, no matter how small, give yourself a pat on the back. This positivity fuels motivation and propels you forward.

Principle 2: Consistency is Key

Dogs thrive on routine, and so do we. Consistency in our habits and actions builds discipline and momentum. Whether it is practicing a new skill or working towards a goal, commit to consistent efforts. Over time, these small daily actions compound into significant results.

Principle 3: Patience and Persistence

Training a dog requires patience and persistence, and so does personal growth. Rome was not built in a day, and neither is a fulfilling life. Embrace setbacks as opportunities to learn and grow stronger. Keep pushing forward, even when the journey feels challenging. The rewards are worth the effort.

Principle 4: Trust the Process

When I train a dog, I trust the training process to yield results. Similarly, trust your own journey towards purpose and passion.

Pawsitivity Unleashed

Trust that each step you take, no matter how small, is leading you towards your destination. Have faith in yourself and the path you are on.

Remember that the journey to finding purpose and passion is not a destination; it is a lifelong adventure. Embrace change as a catalyst for growth. Define your goals, break them down, and take consistent steps forward. Embrace the pawsitive principles of positive reinforcement, consistency, patience, and trust in the process.

Just like training a dog, it is a journey of difficulties, successes, and failures. But through it all, you are not alone. Trust in your potential and believe that you can create a life filled with purpose and passion.

10

Chapter Ten

Embracing Transformation

Finding Purpose to Unleash Your Full Potential

The journey to purpose and passion is a deeply personal and transformative process that often involves various stages of self-discovery and growth. Among these stages, the transformation stage holds particular importance as it marks a significant shift in mindset, behavior, and perspective. Through this stage, you undergo profound changes that propel yourself towards a life filled with meaning, fulfillment, and passion.

Experiencing the Transformation Process in Your Journey

At the heart of any journey towards purpose and passion lies the concept of transformation. This stage represents a pivotal moment when you shed old beliefs, habits, and limitations, and embrace new ways of thinking, being, and living. It is a period of profound change, both internally and externally, that leads to personal growth and self-realization.

Transformation is not a one-time event but rather an ongoing process. It involves a willingness to let go of the familiar and step into the unknown, to confront fears and uncertainties, and to open oneself up to new possibilities. It requires courage, resilience, and a deep commitment to personal development.

Valuable Lessons During a Transformational Journey

As a dog trainer and transformational life coach, I have witnessed firsthand the power of transformation in both animals and humans. In training animals, I have seen how a shift in approach and mindset can lead to remarkable changes in behavior. The same principles apply to our own lives.

Just like training a dog to respond to positive reinforcement, we can train our minds to focus on the positive aspects of life. By adopting a mindset of optimism, gratitude, and resilience, we can overcome obstacles and setbacks with grace and determination.

Heidi, my faithful companion, has been instrumental in my own journey of transformation. She has taught me the importance of consistency, patience, and trust. Through our experiences together, I have learned to embrace change, adapt to new situations, and stay true to my values and goals.

The Significance of Purpose and Passion

At the heart of the transformation stage is the quest for purpose and passion. Purpose gives our lives meaning and direction, while passion fuels our drive and motivation. These are not fleeting emotions but deep-seated desires that guide our choices and actions.

When we are aligned with our purpose and passionate about our pursuits, life takes on a new dimension of richness and fulfillment. We become more focused, energized, and enthusiastic about the path ahead. Challenges are no longer obstacles but opportunities for growth and learning.

Embracing Change and Growth

The transformation stage is not always easy. It requires us to step out of our comfort zones, confront our fears, and embrace change. It may involve letting go of old beliefs and patterns that no longer serve us, and adopting new ones that align with our true selves.

Pawsitivity Unleashed

However, it is through these challenges that we grow and evolve. Every obstacle we overcome, every fear we face, and every lesson we learn brings us closer to our purpose and passion. It is a journey of self-discovery and self-mastery, where we become the architects of our own destiny.

The Role of Resilience & Persistence

Resilience and persistence are key qualities that accompany the transformation stage. They enable us to weather the storms, bounce back from setbacks, and stay committed to our goals. Just as a dog learns new tricks through consistent practice, we too must stay dedicated to our personal growth journey.

There will be times when doubt creeps in, when obstacles seem insurmountable, and when we want to give up. It is during these moments that our resilience is tested, and our commitment to our purpose is reaffirmed. With each setback, we learn valuable lessons that strengthen our resolve.

Cultivating Mindset & Mindfulness

Mindset plays a crucial role in the transformation stage. A growth mindset, characterized by a belief in one's ability to learn and grow, is essential for embracing change and overcoming challenges. It is about seeing setbacks as opportunities for growth and viewing failures as steppingstones to success.

Pawsitivity Unleashed

Mindfulness is another powerful tool for transformation. By staying present in the moment and cultivating awareness of our thoughts and emotions, we gain clarity and insight into our inner workings. This allows us to make conscious choices and act with intention, rather than reacting impulsively.

Celebrating Successes & Milestones

Throughout the transformation stage, it is important to celebrate successes and milestones, no matter how small. These moments of achievement serve as reminders of our progress and growth. They also fuel our motivation and inspire us to continue moving forward.

Just as I celebrate Heidi's progress in training, we must celebrate our own achievements on the journey to purpose and passion. Whether it is completing a challenging task, overcoming a fear, or making a positive change in our lives, each success is a testament to our strength and determination.

Embracing the Journey

The transformation stage is a vital part of the journey to purpose and passion. It is a period of profound change, growth, and self-discovery that leads us towards a more meaningful and fulfilling life. By embracing change, cultivating resilience, and staying true to our purpose, we can navigate this stage with confidence and determination.

Through the lens of training animals and coaching lives, I have come to appreciate the importance of this transformative process. Just as I have witnessed the remarkable changes in animals and clients, I have also experienced my own transformation. Heidi, my loyal companion, has been my guide and inspiration throughout this journey.

As you embark on your own journey of transformation, remember that change is a constant and growth is a lifelong process. Embrace the challenges, celebrate the successes, and stay committed to your purpose and passion. The transformation stage may be challenging, but it is also incredibly rewarding. It is where we discover our true selves, unleash our potential, and create a life filled with purpose and passion.

My Personal Transformation

My journey of reinvention and rediscovery, as I had explained early on, began with a deep longing for something more in my life. Despite my success as a single mother at the time, I had always felt a nagging sense of emptiness. It was as if I was living someone else's life, making decisions based on fear and the need for financial security rather than following my true passions and desires. The path of safety and stability had been my compass for so long that I had lost sight of what truly ignited my soul.

As a single mother, my priority had always been the well-being and security of my family. Every decision I made was filtered through the lens of providing a stable and secure life for my son, Ryan. While these decisions were necessary and responsible, they often came at the expense of my own dreams and aspirations. Any inklings of pursuing my true passions were dismissed as impractical or frivolous, overshadowed by the weight of responsibility.

But beneath the facade of stability and routine, there was a subtle simmering beneath the surface. I felt a disconnect from the vibrant, passionate person I once was, full of dreams and aspirations. The spark that once ignited my soul seemed to have dimmed over the years of prioritizing safety and practicality.

As a child, I had dreamed of endless possibilities, waiting eagerly to grow up and become whatever I wanted to be. Yet, somewhere along the way, those dreams had been buried under layers of responsibility and societal expectations. I had become complacent, settling for a life that was comfortable but lacked true fulfillment.

The turning point came when I realized that the life, I was living was not aligned with my authentic self. I yearned for a sense of purpose and passion that went beyond the daily grind. It was time to break free from the constraints of fear and practicality, to rediscover the dreams and aspirations that had been buried deep within my heart.

Heidi's arrival into my life was a catalyst for this transformation. Her presence brought a renewed sense of joy and vitality, reminding me of the importance of living in the present moment. Watching her navigate the world with curiosity and enthusiasm sparked something within me – a longing to reconnect with the passions and dreams that had lain dormant for too long.

Slowly, I began to peel away the layers of fear and insecurity that had held me back. I allowed myself to dream again, to envision a life filled with purpose and meaning. With Heidi by my side, I took the first steps towards reinventing myself, towards rediscovering the essence of who I truly was.

It was not an easy journey. There were moments of doubt and uncertainty, moments when I questioned whether I was making the right choices. But with each step forward, I felt a renewed sense of energy and purpose. I started to explore new interests and hobbies, stepping outside of my comfort zone and embracing the unknown.

Through it all, Heidi was my constant companion and source of inspiration. Her unwavering love and loyalty reminded me of the courage and resilience within myself. She taught me to live with an open heart, to embrace change and uncertainty as opportunities for growth.

As I look back on my journey of reinvention and rediscovery, I am filled with gratitude for the lessons learned and the growth experienced. I have reconnected with the passions and dreams that once seemed out of reach, and I am pursuing them with a newfound sense of purpose and determination.

Heidi's role in this journey cannot be overstated. She was more than just a dog; she was a symbol of hope and transformation. Her presence in my life brought me a sense of joy and wonder that had been missing for too long. Through her, I rediscovered the power of living authentically, of following my heart's true desires.

Today, I stand tall as a testament to the power of reinvention and rediscovery. I have embraced the uncertainties of life with open arms, knowing that each new challenge is an opportunity for growth. I am no longer the mime in the glass box, pressing against the walls of fear and limitation. Instead, I am free to explore, to dream, and to live a life filled with purpose and passion.

Heidi is a constant reminder of the transformation that is possible when we listen to the whispers of our souls. She taught me that it is never too late to reinvent us, to rediscover the dreams that have been buried within us. And for that, I will be forever grateful.

Pawsitivity Unleashed

Recognizing the Call for Change

It was a quiet realization that whispered to me in moments of solitude: I needed to make a change. Just as I observe subtle cues in the behavior of the dogs I train, I begin to tune in to the subtle signals within myself. It was time for a transformation, a shift in my life that felt both daunting and exhilarating. But I did not know where to start. I felt like a mime in a glass box, pressing against the clear walls, visible to everyone but unable to find an exit. I was stuck in a cycle of routine, unsure of how to break free.

The feeling of being trapped within my own circumstances grew stronger with each passing day. I could see the world moving around me, yet I felt disconnected and uncoordinated. It was as though I was living on autopilot, going through the motions without truly being present.

As a dog trainer, I know the importance of recognizing behavioral patterns and adjusting to achieve desired outcomes. I realized that the same principles could be applied to my own life. I needed to break free from the patterns that held me back, to find a new path forward.

But the first step seemed elusive. I did not have all the answers, and the fear of the unknown held me in its grip. What if I made the wrong choice? What if I failed? These doubts and uncertainties swirled in my mind, creating a barrier to change.

Pawsitivity Unleashed

It was during this time of introspection and uncertainty that Heidi entered my life. Her arrival was serendipitous, a gentle reminder that sometimes the answers we seek come in unexpected forms. As I spent time with her, I began to see the parallels between her journey and mine. Just as she had overcome challenges and found a new lease on life, I too needed to find the courage to step outside of my comfort zone.

Heidi's presence brought a sense of clarity and purpose. She was a symbol of resilience and adaptability, qualities that I needed to cultivate within myself. Watching her navigate the world with enthusiasm and curiosity reminded me of the potential for growth and change that existed within me.

With Heidi by my side, I began to take small steps towards transformation. I started to explore new interests and hobbies, pushing myself out of my comfort zone. Each day brought new challenges, but also new opportunities for growth and self-discovery.

Slowly but surely, the walls of the glass box began to fade away. I no longer felt trapped by my circumstances; instead, I saw them as opportunities for growth and learning. I embraced the uncertainty of the unknown, knowing that true transformation often requires stepping into the unfamiliar.

Pawsitivity Unleashed

Through Heidi's gentle guidance and unwavering companionship, I found the courage to pursue my passions and dreams. I realized that change is not always easy, but it is necessary for growth. Just as I help the dogs, I train to overcome obstacles and achieve their full potential, I too was on a journey of self-discovery and empowerment.

Looking back, I am grateful for the pivotal role that Heidi has played in my life. She has been more than just a rescue dog; she was the catalyst for change and a beacon of hope. Her presence reminded me of the power of resilience, determination, and the importance of listening to the whispers of our hearts.

As I continue my journey of transformation, I still have Heidi by my side. She taught me that even in moments of uncertainty, there is always a path forward. It may not always be clear, but with courage and determination, we can break free from the confines of our glass boxes and embrace the limitless possibilities that await us.

Seeking Inspiration

I was searching for inspiration, seeking answers to questions that seemed to linger in the air, and as often happens, inspiration came from the most unexpected of places. For me, it came in the form of Heidi, a fluffy black 45lb standard poodle with soulful eyes and a gentle spirit. The journey to rescue her was no small feat – a four-hour drive there, and six hours back. But from the moment our eyes met, I felt a profound connection, as if she understood the path I was about to embark upon.

The drive to the rescue was filled with anticipation and excitement, yet also a sense of serenity. I was about to meet a new companion, one who would bring light and joy into my life in ways I could not yet imagine. As I arrived at the location and laid eyes on Heidi for the first time, I was struck by her presence. Her eyes held ancient wisdom, and her gentle demeanor drew me in.

We spent some time getting to know each other both inside and outdoors, surrounded by the sounds of barking dogs and the rustle of leaves in the wind. Despite the chaos around us, there was a quiet understanding between us. It was as though Heidi had been waiting for me, just as I had been searching for her.

Driving back home with Heidi by my side, I could not shake the feeling that this was the beginning of something truly special. The journey was long, but it passed in a blur of excited chatter and the occasional glance at each other as she sat comfortably and calmly in the back seat on my lap, her eyes fixed on me and my mom driving us and Ryan home.

As we settled into our new life together, I discovered that Heidi was more than just a dog – she was a kindred spirit, a companion on my journey of self-discovery and growth. Her presence brought a sense of calm and purpose into my life. She was my constant companion, whether we were exploring new trails in the woods or simply sitting together in quiet contemplation.

In Heidi, I found inspiration, guidance, and unwavering loyalty. She became my confidante, my sounding board, and my greatest source of comfort. With her by my side, I felt a newfound sense of courage to face the challenges that life presented.

Looking back, I realize that Heidi was not just a rescue dog – she rescued me in more ways than I can count. Our journey together was filled with love, laughter, and countless adventures. She taught me the importance of living in the present moment, of cherishing each day as a precious gift.

As we drove back from the rescue that day, I knew deep in my heart that I had found my soulmate in Heidi. Our connection was deeper than words could express, a silent understanding that transcended time and space. She was not just a standard poodle; she was my guardian angel, my guiding light.

And so, our journey together began – a journey of love, friendship, and endless possibilities. Heidi, with her soulful eyes and gentle spirit, had found her way into my heart, and I knew that I was forever changed because of her.

Valuable Life Lessons Taught by A Canine

Lesson 1: The Power of Connection

Heidi showed me that genuine connection transcends words. It is the silent bond that intertwines two souls. Through our shared moments, I came to see her not just as a dog but as a reflection, echoing the potential within myself. If you have ever encountered the notion that dogs and their owners adopt similar traits, you will understand this deeply. With time, boundaries blur, and we subtly morph into one another. Worries and anxieties became intertwined. Her fears and anxieties became my own. It became clear to me that I needed to invest in her well-being.

As Heidi's companion, I felt her joys and fears as if they were my own. When she wagged her tail with excitement, I could not help but feel my spirit lift. And when she cowered during thunderstorms, my heart would ache with empathy. Our connection went beyond the physical; it was a merging of our emotional worlds.

It was not just a one-way street. Just as Heidi influenced me, I could see how my actions and energy affected her. When I was stressed, she would sense it and become more anxious. But when I approached our time together with calmness and positivity, she responded kindly. It was a symbiotic relationship, each of us influencing the other in profound ways.

Pawsitivity Unleashed

Through Heidi, I learned the importance of investing in her well-being. This meant more than just providing food and shelter; it meant nurturing her emotional and mental health. I sought out ways to reduce her anxieties and fears, whether through gentle training methods or creating a safe and comforting environment for her. Seeing her flourish under my care brought me immense joy and fulfillment.

Investing in Heidi's well-being also meant investing in our bond. We spent countless hours together, exploring new places, playing games, and simply enjoying each other's company. These moments of connection were priceless, reinforcing the deep bond we shared.

In return, Heidi gave me unwavering loyalty and unconditional love. She was my confidante, my source of comfort, and my constant companion. Her presence filled my life with warmth and purpose.

As I reflect on our journey together, I am reminded of the profound impact Heidi had on my life. She taught me the true meaning of empathy, compassion, and unconditional love. Our bond transcended words, a silent understanding that brought us closer together.

Through Heidi, I learned that investing in the well-being of those we love is a powerful act of love and compassion. It is about nurturing their physical, emotional, and mental health, creating a foundation for a strong and enduring bond. Heidi's legacy lives on in the love and care I continue to give to those around me, a testament to the profound impact of our connection.

Lesson 2: Setting Intentions

Heidi's love for life is infectious. She still has the same playful energy as she did seven years ago, chasing after tennis balls with endless enthusiasm. Despite her epilepsy, we found ways to manage it naturally, reducing her anxieties and allowing her to live fully. Through her resilience, she taught me to slow down and savor the moments rather than rush through them.

Just as I set clear training goals for Heidi, I began to realize the need to set intentions for my own life. These intentions were not rigid plans but guiding lights that directed my path. I wanted to live with purpose, embracing each moment with gratitude. Heidi's example inspired me to cultivate a mindset of positivity and appreciation. In her eyes, I saw the reflection of a life lived fully, with love and gratitude at its core.

As we journeyed together, I learned to cherish the simple joys: the warmth of the sun on our backs during walks, the sound of her playful barks echoing through the park, and the quiet moments of companionship on lazy afternoons. Heidi's unwavering love and

Pawsitivity Unleashed

resilience taught me to find beauty in every moment, to be present, and to live with an open heart.

Lesson 3: Embracing Gratitude

Heidi's presence taught me the importance of gratitude. Each day, as we explored the world together, I found myself filled with a sense of awe and appreciation. Whether it was the beauty of a sunrise painting the sky in hues of pink and gold or the gentle wag of her tail as she greeted me, there was always something to be grateful for.

What struck me most about Heidi was her resilience and unwavering spirit. She had overcome so much in such a short time. Despite her challenges, she approached life with a sense of joy and energy that was truly inspiring. She welcomed every person who entered our home with open arms and a wagging tail, embodying unconditional love and acceptance.

I witnessed this especially with my then three-year-old son, Ryan. Heidi was gentle and kind to him, nurturing him with her presence and showering him with affection. She understood his innocence and vulnerability, and she became his steadfast companion in play and exploration. I watched as they chased each other around the living room, Ryan's laughter filling the air and Heidi's tail wagging in delight.

Pawsitivity Unleashed

Even after the car accident that led her to multiple surgeries and now arthritis in her front feet, Heidi never let it dampen her spirit. She continued to love life with a fervor that was unmatched. She still reveled in her favorite activities, particularly squirrel hunting and her love for tennis balls. Those bright green orbs kept her busy for hours, her energy boundless.

With her epilepsy, it was just another challenge to overcome. But we found ways to manage it naturally, reducing her anxieties and controlling her seizures. Through it all, Heidi remained resilient and determined. She showed me the power of perseverance and the importance of finding solutions rather than dwelling on problems.

Her ability to live in the moment was a lesson. Heidi never rushed through life; she savored every sniff, every wag, every ball toss. She taught me to slow down and appreciate the simple joys that surround us. In her gratitude for each day, I found a deeper appreciation for the moments that make life truly meaningful.

As the years passed, Heidi's energy may have slowed a bit, but her spirit remained as vibrant as ever. She may not chase tennis balls with the same gusto as she did seven years ago, but her love for life continues to shine through. Her presence in our home is a constant reminder to be grateful for the love and joy that surrounds us, even in the face of challenges.

Pawsitivity Unleashed

Heidi's journey taught me more about gratitude than any book or lecture ever could. Her unwavering love, resilience, and zest for life are qualities I strive to embody every day. She may have been my faithful companion, but in many ways, she was also my greatest teacher.

Lesson 4: Living in the Moment

Like Heidi and most dogs, they have an innate ability to live fully in the present moment. Heidi was no exception. She reminded me to let go of worries about the past or future and simply enjoy the now. Whether we were playing fetch in the park or cuddling on the couch, she was always fully present. Her zest for life was contagious, and she brought a sense of joy and spontaneity to every moment.

When I got home, life was full because of her and my son. It was the best part of our day. Ryan was only three at the time, and he still had that great belly laugh that young children have. Standard poodles tend to be silly and playful, and she could always make him laugh so hard. We would play for hours with her in the living room and then outside and then back in the living room. She loved to wrestle and chase the tennis ball, her tail wagging furiously all the while.

Ryan loved to make videos of her antics with my cell phone. Those days as a single mom before I met my husband were long, hard, and busy. But Heidi made it all better. Her presence brought a sense of peace and happiness to our home. Even on the toughest days, her wagging tail and playful antics could lift our spirits.

As the sun set outside our window, casting a warm glow over our living room, I would watch Ryan and Heidi play together. Their laughter filled the air, a beautiful symphony of joy. In those precious moments, I felt grateful for the love and happiness they brought into our lives.

Heidi was not just a pet; she was a cherished member of our family. Her unconditional love and playful spirit enriched our days and created memories that I will always hold dear. She taught me the importance of living in the moment, finding joy in simple pleasures, and appreciating the love that surrounds us.

Even now, years later, I can still feel the warmth of those evenings spent playing with Heidi and Ryan. They were moments of pure happiness and connection, moments that I will always treasure. Heidi may no longer be with us, but her spirit lives on in the laughter and love she brought into our home.

Celebrating Success Together

As Heidi and I worked towards our respective goals, we celebrated every small victory along the way. Whether it was mastering a new trick or making a breakthrough in my own life, we marked these moments with joy and gratitude. These celebrations were not just about the achievement itself; they were a recognition of our progress and the bond we shared.

Our little victories became cherished milestones on our journey. When Heidi learned to paw my arm for a potty break or when I completed a challenging task in my personal growth, we would pause to revel in the moment. The wag of Heidi's tail and the sparkle in her eyes mirrored the joy in my heart.

Through these celebrations, I learned the power of positive reinforcement not only for Heidi but also for myself. Each small success reinforced our motivation and strengthened our connection. It was a cycle of growth and appreciation that fueled our journey forward.

These moments of celebration also taught me the importance of mindfulness. Instead of rushing through life's achievements, we took the time to savor them. We embraced the present moment, basking in the joy of our accomplishments.

As we continued our path, our celebrations became more than just markers of progress. They became reminders of our resilience and determination. No challenge seemed insurmountable when we approached it with a positive mindset and a shared sense of purpose.

Pawsitivity Unleashed

I encourage you to celebrate your own victories, no matter how small they may seem. Whether it is mastering a new skill, overcoming a fear, or simply taking a step towards your goals, pause to acknowledge and appreciate your progress. In these moments of celebration, you will find the motivation and strength to keep moving forward on your journey of growth and discovery.

My Top 5 Principles from My Own Transformation

Principle 1: Consistency

Consistency played a crucial role for both Heidi and me. In her training sessions and in my personal growth, staying consistent was key to our progress. After the first year, I transitioned Heidi to a new natural diet, and we made the decision to avoid certain unnecessary vaccines that we believed were triggering her epilepsy. With sufficient daily exercise and the new diet, her anxiety vanished. Remarkably, after a year on the new diet, we had not experienced any seizures either. Remaining steadfast and consistent, it has now been five years since we last saw any seizures.

I applied the same principle of consistency to train her in new skills, and we often embarked on joyful rides together. Through consistent training, she learned to paw my arm to signal when she needed a potty break. Remarkably, she has successfully accompanied me on 1000-mile road trips over twenty times without any issues, all thanks to our consistent training.

Just as I used consistent methods to teach Heidi new behaviors, I applied the same principle to my own habits and routines. When I began my personal growth journey, I integrated exercises into my daily routine. I found joy in daily affirmations and regular journaling. Over time, these seemingly small changes accumulated into significant transformations.

Principle 2: Positive Reinforcement

Heidi has always been trained using positive reinforcement by me. She responded best to this approach, and I found that I did too. Instead of dwelling on mistakes or setbacks, I focused on celebrating successes, no matter how small. As an athlete, not all coaches shared this methodology. Many times, the approach was to call out negatives, aiming to draw out embarrassment to create change. Some may argue it was effective at the time, but I no longer participate in those sports. The old method often relied on fear and punishment – running miles for mistakes or doing pushups for missed fly balls. But who did that truly benefit?

Some still practicing this approach may claim to see immediate results, and in some cases, they might. However, what are the long-term effects? Often, they do not stick around long enough to find out. Many people trained in this style do not maintain what they have learned. Consequently, positive reinforcement was developed to strengthen behavior and is widely recognized as a more effective and humane approach to behavior modification for both animals and humans.

This is why the positive mindset propelled me and many others I work with forward on their journey.

Principle 3: Adaptability

Life, like dog training, is full of unexpected twists and turns. I learned to be adaptable, adjusting my course, when necessary, without losing sight of my ultimate goals. Heidi's flexibility in learning new tricks inspired me to embrace change with open arms.

Principle 4: Trust in the Journey

In training a dog, trust is essential. The same goes for life; trusting in the process and believing in ourselves propels us forward. Heidi taught me to trust in the journey, knowing that each step was leading us closer to our purpose.

A Newfound Sense of Fulfillment & Gratitude

Principle 5: Gratitude

Pawsitivity Unleashed

As I reflect on this transformative time with Heidi by my side, I am filled with gratitude for the lessons learned. Through the lens of dog training, I found a path to reinvention and rediscovery. Heidi, my faithful companion, was not just a dog but a guide on this journey.

Together, we celebrated success with pawsitive principles that are transferable to life. By embracing the lessons of connection, intention, gratitude, and living in the moment, I have unlocked a newfound sense of fulfillment. Purpose and passion are not distant dreams but tangible realities within our grasp.

I encourage you to approach your own journey with the spirit of a dog trainer. Set clear intentions, celebrate every small victory, and trust in the process. Remember, the journey to finding purpose and passion is not a sprint but a joyful exploration with loyal companions by our side.

11

Chapter Eleven

Continuing Your Journey

Embracing the Everlasting Path to Purpose & Passion

The 30-day challenge was just the beginning. It served as a catalyst, a spark that ignited the flame of change within you. As you reflect on the progress made during those thirty days, you realize that transformation is an ongoing process, a journey without a destination. It is about embracing a new way of living, thinking, and being—a journey that extends far beyond the confines of a mere month.

In the whirlwind of the 30-day challenge, you may have experienced moments of clarity, breakthroughs, and newfound passions. You may have felt a renewed sense of purpose, a deeper

Pawsitivity Unleashed

connection with yourself, and a surge of motivation to create the life you desire. These glimpses of transformation are powerful, but they are just the beginning.

The true essence of change lies in the continuation of the work you have started. It is about integrating the lessons learned, the practices cultivated, and the mindset embraced into your daily life. It is about making a conscious decision to prioritize your growth, well-being, and happiness each day, even when the initial excitement of the challenge fades.

One of the most important reasons to continue your work past the 30-day challenge is the realization that transformation is not linear. It is not a one-time event or a quick fix. It is a journey filled with difficulties, twists and turns, successes, and setbacks. By committing to ongoing growth and development, you are better equipped to navigate these fluctuations with grace and resilience.

Moreover, continuing your work allows you to deepen your understanding of yourself. The more you explore, reflect, and engage in self-discovery, the clearer your path becomes. You uncover layers of your being, untangle limiting beliefs, and discover hidden passions and talents. It is a process of constant evolution, where each day brings new insights and revelations.

Another crucial aspect of continuing your work is the reinforcement of positive habits and practices. Just as muscles grow stronger with consistent exercise, your mind and spirit flourish with regular nourishment. Whether it is daily meditation, journaling, gratitude practices, or setting aside time for self-care, these rituals become anchors in the stormy seas of life. They provide stability, grounding, and a sense of purpose amidst the chaos.

Beyond personal growth, continuing your work also benefits those around you. As you become a beacon of positivity, resilience, and purpose, you inspire others to do the same. Your energy and enthusiasm are contagious, creating a ripple effect of positivity in your relationships, work, and community. By being the best version of yourself, you inadvertently become a source of light for others.

Moreover, the journey of reinvention and recreation is not just about personal fulfillment; it is about creating a life of meaning and contribution. As you delve deeper into your purpose and passion, you uncover ways to serve others, make a difference, and leave a legacy. Whether it is through volunteering, mentoring, starting a passion project, or pursuing a meaningful career, your journey becomes intertwined with the greater good.

It is also important to acknowledge that continuing your work requires patience and persistence. There will be days when motivation wanes, when old habits resurface, and when life throws unexpected challenges your way. In these moments, it is crucial to remember why you started this journey in the first place. Reconnect with your vision, your goals, and the feelings of empowerment and joy that come with living authentically.

Additionally, surrounding yourself with a supportive community is essential for sustained growth. Seek out like-minded individuals who uplift and inspire you. Share your journey, celebrate your wins, and lean on others for support when needed. A strong support system can provide encouragement, accountability, and fresh perspectives on your path.

As you continue your work past the 30-day challenge, remember that self-compassion is key. Be gentle with yourself on this journey of growth and transformation. Embrace the inevitable difficulties as opportunities for learning and growth. Celebrate your progress, no matter how small, and forgive yourself for any setbacks.

Ways to Continue on After Your 30-Day Challenge

Embrace Consistency

Consistency is key to maintaining the progress you have made during your 30-day journey. Just as I have used consistent methods to train dogs in new behaviors, consistency in our daily practices is crucial for long-term growth. This may include daily affirmations, journaling, or engaging in activities that bring joy and fulfillment.

Cultivate Mindfulness

Pawsitivity Unleashed

Living in the moment and being mindful of our thoughts and actions is essential for pawsitive living. Practicing mindfulness allows you to become aware of your emotions, reactions, and behaviors, empowering you to make conscious choices aligned with your values and goals. This can be as simple as taking a few minutes each day to focus on your breath or practicing gratitude for the present moment.

Share Your Journey

Sharing your experiences and insights with others not only reinforces your own learning but also inspires and uplifts those around you. As a dog trainer and life coach, I have seen the power of sharing stories and connecting with others on similar paths. Whether through writing, speaking engagements, or simply having meaningful conversations, sharing your journey can create a ripple effect of pawsitivity in the world.

Practice Self-Care

Prioritizing self-care is essential for sustaining a pawsitive life. Just as I prioritize the well-being of the animals I train, it is important to prioritize your own physical, mental, and emotional health. This may include regular exercise, adequate rest, healthy nutrition, and engaging in activities that bring joy and relaxation.

Set Meaningful Goals

Setting goals that align with your values and passions gives us direction and purpose in your journey. These goals serve as guideposts, helping you stay focused and motivated. Whether it is pursuing a new hobby, starting a passion project, or deepening connections with loved ones, setting meaningful goals keeps you inspired and engaged in your pawsitive living journey.

Embrace Resilience

The path to living a pawsitive life is not without challenges and setbacks. Just as dogs learn from their mistakes and continue to grow, we too must embrace resilience in the face of adversity. It is through overcoming challenges that we discover our strength and resilience, leading to personal growth and transformation.

Your journey towards living a pawsitive life extends far beyond the initial 30-day path. It is a lifelong commitment to growth, self-discovery, and connection. Through my own experiences as a dog trainer and life coach, I have learned that embracing the pawsitive principles is not just a temporary endeavor; it is a way of life.

By continuing to cultivate consistency, mindfulness, learning, sharing, self-care, goal setting, and resilience, you can sustain the pawsitive changes initiated during the initial journey. It is my hope that by sharing my story and these insights, you and others may find inspiration and guidance on their own journey towards living a purposeful and passionate life.

As you embark on this continued journey, let us remember the words of Mahatma Gandhi: "Be the change that you wish to see in the world." By living a pawsitive life, we not only transform ourselves but also contribute to a more pawsitive and harmonious world for all beings.

Pawsitivity Unleashed

Closing Thoughts a Special Message from Kristin

Dearest Esteemed Reader,

As we stand on the threshold of continued growth, let us embrace the enduring truth that the path to rediscovery, reinvention, and reclaiming our lives extends far beyond a 30-day challenge. It is a lifelong odyssey, a magnificent expedition into the depths of our potential.

Like the steady hand guiding a dog through training exercises, our commitment to pawsitive habits and behaviors ensures a foundation of resilience and progress. Let us remain steadfast in our pursuit, knowing that each small step forward paves the way for profound transformation.

Amidst the trials and tribulations of life, practicing self-compassion becomes our guiding light. Just as we would gently guide a pup through a learning curve, let us extend the same kindness and understanding to ourselves. Embracing our mistakes and failures as opportunities for growth allows us to navigate challenges with grace and resilience.

Gratitude, like a beacon in the darkness, illuminates our path with its radiant warmth. By pausing each day to acknowledge the blessings that surround us, we shift our perspective from scarcity to abundance. Let us

Pawsitivity Unleashed

288

cultivate a heart overflowing with gratitude, for it is in the simple mo-ments of joy and connection that we find true richness.

Remember, transformation is not a destination but a journey—a magnificent voyage of self-discovery and growth. With each new day, we embark upon a fresh canvas upon which to paint our dreams and aspirations. Let us remain dedicated to our journey, knowing that every step forward brings us closer to our true potential.

I extend my deepest gratitude to you for embarking on this journey of rediscovery and reinvention alongside me. May you continue to harness the boundless power of pawsitivity and inspire others to do the same. Together, let us create a world brimming with love, compassion, and joy—one paw at a time.

And remember, your journey in training is far from over. Stay connected with us through our Facebook Community, follow us on our social media platforms, explore our website, and subscribe to our newsletters. We provide additional resources and support to accompany you on your pet's health and wellness journey.

With boundless love and pawsitivity!

Kristin

Additional Resources

Personal Self Help Resources

- Check out *Pawsitivity Unleashed* Fan Page

- One-On-One Coaching Sessions with Kristin Leest
- o Complete the PVQ40 Values Coaching Assessment
- o Schedule first Initial Free Consultation for One-on-One Coaching Support – Visit www.kristinleest.com to schedule the appointment and book the event.
- Visit www.kristinleest.com to follow my inspirational blog for additional self-help resources.
- Check out Pawsitivity on YouTube, Instagram, Pinterest, Facebook, and Twitter! Links can be found on www.kristinleest.com.
- VIA Institute on Character – *Free VIA Strengths Assessment* www.viacharacter.org

Pet Health & Wellness Resources

- Check out www.powerofpawsitive.com
- Check out Pawsitivity on YouTube, Instagram, Pinterest, Twitter and TikTok. Links are at www.caninepawsitivity.com

Pawsitivity Unleashed

Additional Resources Continued

Pet Health & Wellness Resources

- Check out Power of Pawsitive – Dog training Private Facebook Community
- Read Kristin's Meet me with Pawsitivity – A great resource for dog training with positive reinforcement.
- The Power of Pawsitive can be found on YouTube, Instagram, Pinterest, Facebook, and Twitter! Links are at www.powerofpawsitive.com
- Join the Power of Pawsitive Facebook Fans Page
- Join the Pawsitivity Facebook Fan Page
- Check out the Power of Pawsitive Online Community Center
- Check out the Power of Pawsitive Free Online Resources
- Check out the Power of Pawsitive Free Training Courses
- Become a *Paws Academy Certified Instructor* with Power of Pawsitive

References

Ariely, D. (2008). Predictably Irrational: The Hidden Forces That Shape Our Decisions. HarperCollins.

Ariely, D. (2010). The Upside of Irrationality: The Unexpected Benefits of Defying Logic at Work and at Home. Harper.

Brown, B. (2010). The gifts of imperfection: Let go of who you think you're supposed to be and embrace who you are. Hazelden Publishing.

Brown, B. (2012). Daring greatly: How the courage to be vulnerable transforms the way we live, love, parent, and lead. Avery.

Brown, B. (2018). Dare to lead: Brave work. Tough conversations. Whole hearts. Random House.

Brown, B. (2010). The Gifts of Imperfection: Let Go of Who You Think You're Supposed to Be and Embrace Who You Are. Hazelden Publishing.

Bardi, A., Buchanan, K. E., Goodwin, R., Slabu, L., & Robinson, M. (2014). Value stability and change during self-chosen life transitions: Self-selection versus socialization effects. Journal of Personality and Social Psychology, 106(1), 131–147.

Blatt, S. J., Zuroff, D. C., Hawley, L. L., & Auerbach, J. S. (2010). Predictors of sustained therapeutic change. Psychotherapy Research, 20(1), 37–54. https://doi.org/10.1080/10503300903121094

Cardone, G. (2011). The 10X rule: The only difference between success and failure. Wiley.

Pawsitivity Unleashed

Carnegie, D. (1936). How to win friends and influence people. Simon and Schuster.

Census.gov. (2022, November 17). Census Bureau Releases New Estimates on America's Families and Living Arrangements. Retrieved from https://www.census.gov/newsroom/press-releases/2022/americas-families-and-living-arrangements.html

Character, V. I. (2024, February 11). VIA Institute on Character. Retrieved February 11, 2024, from VIA Institute on Character: https://viacharacter.org/

Christensen, C. M. (2013). The innovator's dilemma: When new technologies cause great firms to fail. Harvard Business Review Press.

Clear, J. (2018). Atomic habits: An easy & proven way to build good habits & break bad ones. Avery.

Collins, J. (2001). Good to great: Why some companies make the leap and others don't. HarperBusiness.

Covey, S. R. (2013). The 7 habits of highly effective people: Powerful lessons in personal change. Simon & Schuster.

Coyle, D. (2009). The Talent Code: Greatness Isn't Born. It's Grown. Here's How. Bantam.

Csikszentmihalyi, M. (1990). Flow: The Psychology of Optimal Experience. Harper & Row.

Doe, A. (2018). Embracing Change: A Guide to Personal Growth. Self-Help Press.

Duckworth, A. (2016). Grit: The power of passion and perseverance. Scribner.

Duckworth, A. (2019). The Power of Passion and Perseverance. Scribner.

Duhigg, C. (2016). Smarter Faster Better: The Secrets of Being Productive in Life and Business. Random House.

Duhigg, C. (2012). The power of habit: Why we do what we do in life and business. Random House.

Dweck, C. S. (2008). Mindset: The new psychology of success. Random House.

Dyer, W. W. (1976). Your Erroneous Zones: Step-by-Step Advice for Escaping the Trap of Negative Thinking and Taking Control of Your Life. HarperCollins.

Elrod, H. (2012). The miracle morning: The not-so-obvious secret guaranteed to transform your life (before 8am). Hal Elrod International.

Ferriss, T. (2009). The 4-hour workweek: Escape 9-5, live anywhere, and join the new rich. Harmony.

Gawande, A. (2014). Being Mortal: Medicine and What Matters in the End. Metropolitan Books.

Gawande, A. (2002). Complications: A Surgeon's Notes on an Imperfect Science. Picador.

Gawande, A. (2010). The Checklist Manifesto: How to Get Things Right. Picador.

Gerber, M. E. (1995). The E-myth revisited: Why most small businesses don't work and what to do about it. HarperCollins.

Gilbert, E. (2006). Eat, Pray, Love: One Woman's Search for Everything Across Italy, India, and Indonesia. Penguin Books.

Gilbert, E. (2015). Big Magic: Creative Living Beyond Fear. Riverhead Books.

Pawsitivity Unleashed

Gladwell, M. (2008). Outliers: The story of success. Little, Brown and Company.

Hardy, D. (2012). The compound effect: Jumpstart your income, your life, your success. Vanguard Press.

Hearts, B. H. (2024, 11 February). Big Hugs for Little Hearts . Retrieved from www.bighugsforlittlehearts.org

Jones, S. (2019). Consistency: The Key to Success. Habits of Excellence Publishing.

Kahneman, D. (2011). Thinking, fast and slow. Farrar, Straus and Giroux.

Keller, G., & Papasan, J. (2013). The one thing: The surprisingly simple truth behind extraordinary results. Bard Press.

Leuty, M. &. (2011). Evidence of construct validity for cork values. Journal of Vocational Behavior, 79(2),379-390.

Lu, Y., Yu, K., & Gan, X. (2022, May 23). Effects of a SMART Goal Setting and 12-Week Core Strength Training Intervention on Physical Fitness and Exercise Attitudes in Adolescents: A Randomized Controlled Trial. International Journal of Enviornmental Reaserch and Public Health , 19(13), 7715. Retrieved March 2024, from MDPI: https://www.mdpi.com/1660-4601/19/13/7715

McKeown, G. (2014). Essentialism: The disciplined pursuit of less. Crown Business.

Newport, C. (2016). Deep Work: Rules for Focused Success in a Distracted World. Grand Central Publishing.

Pawsitivity Unleashed

Patterson, K., Grenny, J., McMillan, R., & Switzler, A. (2011). Crucial conversations: Tools for talking when stakes are high. McGraw-Hill Education.

Pink, D. H. (2011). Drive: The Surprising Truth About What Motivates Us. Riverhead Books.

Pink, D. H. (2018). When: The Scientific Secrets of Perfect Timing. Riverhead Books.

Ries, E. (2011). The lean startup: How today's entrepreneurs use continuous innovation to create radically successful businesses. Currency.

Robbins, A. (1991). Awaken the giant within: How to take immediate control of your mental, emotional, physical and financial destiny! Free Press.

Robbins, A. (2017). Unshakeable: Your financial freedom playbook. Simon & Schuster.

Robbins, A. (2014). Money: Master the game: 7 simple steps to financial freedom. Simon & Schuster.

Rubin, G. (2015). Better Than Before: What I Learned About Making and Breaking Habits--to Sleep More, Quit Sugar, Procrastinate Less, and Generally Build a Happier Life. Broadway Books.

Sinek, S. (2009). Start with why: How great leaders inspire everyone to take action. Portfolio.

Roccas, S., Sagiv, L., & Navon, M. (2017). Methodological Issues in Studying Personal Values. American Psychology Association Journal, 15-50. https://link.springer.com/chapter/10.1007/978-3-319-56352-7_2

Pawsitivity Unleashed

Rubin, G. (2017). The Four Tendencies: The Indispensable Personality Profiles That Reveal How to Make Your Life Better (and Other People's Lives Better, Too). Harmony

Sagiv, L., & Schwartz, S. H. (2022). Personal values across cultures. Annual Review of Psychology, 73, 517–546. https://doi.org/10.1146/annurev-psych-020821-125100

Schwartz, S. H., & Bilsky, W. (1987). Toward a psychological structure of human values. Journal of Personality and Social Psychology, 53, 550–562.

Schwartz, S H. (2017). The Refined Theory of Basic Values. American Psychology Association Journal, 51-72. https://link.springer.com/chapter/10.1007/978-3-319-56352-7_3

Schwartz, S. e. (2001). Extending the cross-cultural validity of the theory of basic human values with different method of measurement. Journal of Cross-cultural Psychology,, 32(5),519-542.

Schwartz, S. H. (2012, 12). An Overview of the Schwartz Theory of Basic Values. Online Readings in Psychology and Culture, 2(1), p. 2(1). Retrieved February 12, 2024, from https://doi.org/10.9707/2307-0919.1116

Schwartz, S. H. (1994). Are there universal aspects in the structure and contents of human values? Journal of Social Issues, 50, 19–45.

Schwartz, S. H. (2012). An overview of the Schwartz theory of basic values. Online Reading in Psychology and Culture, 2(1), Article no. 11.

Schwartz, S. H. (2009). Draft users manual: Proper use of the Schwarz Value Survey, version 14 January 2009, compiled by R. F. Littrell. Auckland,

Pawsitivity Unleashed

New Zealand: Centre for Cross Cultural Comparisons. Retrieved from http://www.crossculturalcentre.homestead.com

Smith, J. (2020). The Power of Positive Reinforcement in Dog Training. Journal of Canine Behavior, 10(3), 45-59.

Tzu, S. (2005). The art of war. Shambhala Publications.

Thiel, P., & Masters, B. (2014). Zero to one: Notes on startups, or how to build the future. Crown Business.

Thaler, R. H. (2008). Nudge: Improving Decisions About Health, Wealth, and Happiness. Penguin Books.

Vanderkam, L. (2015). I Know How She Does It: How Successful Women Make the Most of Their Time. Portfolio.

Wong, Q. J. J., & Moulds, M. L. (2011). The relationship between modes of thinking and symptoms of depression and anxiety. Cognitive Therapy and Research, 35(6), 560–566. https://doi.org/10.1007/s10608-011-9379-7

Index

About the Author

Kristin Leest is a remarkable individual who dedicates herself passionately to various causes that are close to her heart.

Not limited to being an author, Kristin also excels as a life coach, dog trainer, and breeder of standard poodles registered with the American Kennel Club. Her life is a vibrant tapestry woven with purpose and commitment to causes associated with children and animals in need.

For the past six years, Kristin has served as the proud Founder and CEO of Big Hugs for Little Hearts, a registered 501(c)(3) nonprofit organization based in Charleston, South Carolina. This organization is devoted to supporting children overcoming abuse, neglect, and abandonment, highlighting Kristin's unwavering dedication to making a positive impact in the lives of young individuals.

In 2023, Kristin embarked on a new venture fueled by her passion for canine health and wellness. She established Pawsitivity, LLC, a company specializing in new-age natural pet nutritional supplements for dogs and cats. Their mission is to provide customized natural nutritional supplements tailored to the individual needs of each pet, aiming to promote vitality, longevity, and enhance the lives of pets worldwide. Additionally, Kristin donates 1% of all her sales to local animal welfare organizations and animal rescues, further expressing her commitment to giving back to the community.

Expanding her repertoire, Kristin has also ventured into the realm of publishing with two heartfelt works. "Meet Me with Pawsitivity: A Comprehensive Guide to Effective Dog Training Through Positive Reinforcement" offers invaluable insights into fostering strong bonds with beloved furry companions, while "Cooking with Chef Ginger and Chef Ruby: Wholesome Tails & Trails Cookie and Dessert Recipes for Your Favorite Pet" is a delightful cookbook crafted with love and care, dedicated to satisfying our pets' taste buds with natural treats made from ingredients found in our kitchens.

Through her roles as CEO, life coach, author, and philanthropist, Kristin Leest endeavors to make a positive impact in the lives of pets and their owners worldwide. Her journey serves as an inspiration, highlighting the importance of uncovering purpose, embracing authenticity, following one's heart, inspiring others, and giving back to the community. These values are the cornerstone of her happiness and success, and she remains steadfast in sharing and inspiring others through her endeavors.

Grab a Sneak Peek

I hope you enjoyed reading **Pawsitivity Unleashed**. *If you have a moment to check out my website,* www.kristinleest.com you can **find more great resources and information** *on upcoming events and more.*

I love to hear from my fans*! If you would like to* **share your thoughts,** please consider **submitting a review on my website, or anywhere you purchased the book**. Good or bad I would love to hear from you! Send me a message at www.kristinleest.com, that you posted a review and as a thank you I will send you an additional gift.

Now, *for that sneak peek I promised…* please go to www.kristinleest.com and *click the link on the first page*. Submit your information and **I will send you a sneak peek** at your email.

Thank you again for taking the time to read **Pawsitivity Unleashed!** Until we meet again, & hopefully soon.

Keep doing you. You got this!